SHOW ME YOURS
& I'LL SHOW YOU MINE

SHOW ME YOURS & I'LL SHOW YOU MINE

RACHEL HOSPERS

gatekeeper press

Columbus, Ohio

Show Me Yours And I'll Show You Mine

Published by Gatekeeper Press
2167 Stringtown Rd, Suite 109
Columbus, OH 43123-2989
www.GatekeeperPress.com

The cover design, interior formatting, typesetting, and editorial work for this book are entirely the product of the author. Gatekeeper Press did not participate in and is not responsible for any aspect of these elements.

ISBN (hardcover): 9781642378405
eISBN: 9781642378412

For my parents, my Snapchat friends,
and my soul mates.

And for my dog.

Table of Amazing Content

Introduction

You may be asking yourself, what the hell am I doing reading a book written by a twenty-three-year-old? I say, great question. If I were you, I would definitely not pick up a book written by someone young, hot, and seemingly uninteresting. Here's the kicker, though. I *would* read something written by me. As a matter of fact, I do daily! I am unwaveringly dedicated to rereading old tweets of mine that I still find absolutely hilarious, if I do say so myself. In addition to my social media addiction, there are a few things you should know about me before diving into the unfiltered, raw, emotional war zone that is my mind. You are holding a book not only written by a twenty-three-year-old, but also by a struggling artist on the relentless feat of making her dreams of becoming a professional dancer (and now author, apparently) come true. No, I am not a stripper, so save your jokes and hold up before you scoff at my lack of qualifications. I have reason to believe there may be something of value for you ahead. My Snapchat friends seem to think so at least.

You heard me right. Amidst my frenzy of Snapchat posts— proving to be a coping mechanism for suppressed breakup heartache—and an eating disorder that was growing worse by the day, I found myself facedown on my white duvet in my tiny rented room in North Hollywood, staring with disbelief at my little blue screen. Tears welled in my eyes as I read a message from an old acquaintance informing me that my goofy, self-reflective posts had provided her with comfort throughout a difficult time in her life. I felt warmth in my chest, followed by excitement bubbling up in my stomach. I had been launching fragments of my mind out into nothingness for pure selfish relief and unknowingly, the material had resonated with someone.

Soon after that conversation, I began pounding away at my keyboard, expanding on the ideas I had been posting about over the past few months. Only six weeks later, I bore messy, unbrushed hair, and a first draft of my regurgitated thoughts gleamed loud and proud in a Microsoft Word document. What I thought were dumb, meaningless jokes became themes for significant subjects in my life. By mapping out my mind, I was able to dig deeper than ever before.

Inviting you along for this ride was one of my more terrifying ideas, but I felt as though not sharing my findings about myself would be straight-up wrong because this inward research damn near saved my life. You see, I am not here to pretend I have all the solutions to your ever-expanding list of problems, you hot mess express! I am not even necessarily here to give you earth-shattering advice. This is not a self-help book. If you are searching for one of those, I am confident you can locate one nearby authored by someone with outstanding credentials. (I will offer recommendations about some of my favorites in the back of this book.)

But please, stay here. Do not leave! I crave your attention and your validation! Pardon me. For a moment there I had you mistaken for a six-foot-something brown-haired man with nice facial hair and a wandering eye (don't you worry, we will get there).

As you may be able to tell, I have a decent sense of humor and I genuinely believe you can learn a thing or two about yourself while reading about my life. Together we will sift through the men who have made me cry and what I have learned from them and the world around me. We will trace back to the crucial beginning of my development and question the patterns that have tripped me up and caused me a great deal of pain until now. I have a feeling you will able to take a look at my pathetic mistakes and once you have stopped laughing at them, you may accrue the knowledge about how not to make them the same way I did. I also hope that some of your issues reveal themselves right in front of your eyes and push you to explore the workings of your own mind. Let's face it; you might be better off than me. But I'll save you the suspense: you are not perfect either. So, no, this is not a self-help book backed by intelligent psychological studies conducted in a lab. I like to consider what you are holding to be a memoir of self-reflection supported by life, learning, breakups, friendships, tears, beginnings, endings, and dream-chasing, powered by cashews and lots and lots of cold brew.

So, back to your question: *what the hell am I doing reading a book by a twenty-three-year-old?* What are you looking at me for? I have no clue. You obviously need to gaze inward and figure that out for yourself! Okay, let's get started then, shall we?

Chapter One

Why is Marvin Gaye's "Let's Get it On" Playing at Urgent Care?

I have a tendency to lean towards living a life of extremes. But no, not how you might assume. I am not even close to being rad enough to be racing cars, flying planes, or surfing giant waves off the shores of Bali. You are more likely to find me locked in my house for weeks, not sleeping, not responding to emails, overconsuming almond butter, hunched over my laptop because I had a bright idea to write a book. Sexy, right? Where is my Tinder photo of me sitting here in the sweatpants I haven't changed out of in days?

If I am in my quote unquote healthy routine of everyday life in Los Angeles, I am eating avocados, exercising daily, drinking protein shakes, taking my multivitamins, getting eight hours of sleep, and almost never allowing myself even a single cocktail. But if I am on vacation in Italy, you can find me at the bar making out with the cute bartender who does not speak a lick of English, taking shots with strangers, staying up until the sun rises, only to finish the night off with an entire pizza to myself. I rarely allow myself to purchase ice cream at the grocery store, but when I do, you better believe that pint has vanished by the morning. Without even thinking about it, my television's remote will have gathered dust for a month and a half but then, before you can say "Netflix 'n chill," I have binge-watched five seasons of Grey's Anatomy in one weekend, again. I either eat ten servings of vegetables in a day or none for a week. One day, I am a sap, crying to Taylor Swift love songs in my room. But the next day, you could pull up next to me in traffic and witness some pretty epic headbanging to a Kanye West jam about hoes. I am either unapologetically single, independent, and in tune with my desires, or I am wholly invested in the needs and wishes of the person I am in love with to the point that who I am gets completely dissolved in the mix.

Ding ding ding! I know this is all painfully adorable, but are we beginning to see the problem here, folks? I am not saying I do not love every side of my personality because I truly do. But a dispute arises for me because leading a life that bounces back and forth from one extreme to another is not sustainable over the long-term and is likely the cause of my chronic migraines and a few other *cough* threats to my well-being, such as my unhealthy need for male approval and my extreme compulsion to punish myself. Some ebb and flow is healthy in life and choosing to be rigidly one way all the time is just as unnatural as being a respected Catholic priest on a Sunday morning after attending a gay sex club the night before. (Hey, I think this behavior should be allowed, celebrated even, but I do not make the rules.)

Committing to one steady lane would be a disservice to the organized, disciplined parts of me and also to the reckless, carefree parts of me. I need both! What I am striving for is a healthy equilibrium of all compounds of myself in order to create a daily life that is productive, enjoyable, and authentic to who I am. Call it balance. Call it the yin and the yang of life. Whatever you have to do to keep yourself out of urgent care. For clarity, in this chapter I will refer to my strict, rigid identity as "Nine-to-Five Rach" and my fun-loving, cool identity as "Weekend Rach." I appreciate the thought, but no, you do not have to call the psych ward on me just yet. Bear with me here.

We are creatures of habit and routine. A steady environment breeds steady brain chemical composition, which in turn causes health, order, and peace. I operate optimally when my life has a fixed rhythm, but I also work alarmingly well in states of high-stakes adrenaline. Earlier this year, I became cognizant of the fact that my adrenaline addiction was driving my actions more than I knew. My family has an intense history of addiction, but thankfully I never got hooked on booze or drugs. Nope, adrenaline is my vice of choice. Possibly unattainable men and chocolate too. Significantly less cinematic than venturing down a dark alley for drugs, you can find me on my couch scrolling through to see who viewed my Instagram story, scrounging for my hit.

I have been told time and time again to avoid men who make me feel an adrenaline rush. Those people are probably right, and you should one hundred percent run for cover if anyone is ever waving the same bright shiny red flags this particular man was to me last year. A mixture of cortisol (the stress hormone) and adrenaline would pulse through my veins while he was en route to my house. One sunny morning, I was on a peaceful walk with my dog, enjoying a podcast in the crisp, mild LA winter air when his name popped up on my phone. My stomach hit the floor as I read the words "I want to see uuuuu."

My friends, I advise you not to date a guy who makes you feel this way. Relationships should enhance our lives, right? We should aim for healthy romantic encounters that bring us more joy than they do pain, right? Right. Inconsistency from a partner is a giant red flag. Sure, it is intoxicating when they grant you that lovely attention, but it feels like hell when they withhold it. We should seek partners that make us feel steadily positive overall. Extreme highs and lows are not an indication of a healthy partnership.

Last year I found myself coming out of a long-term, mutually nurturing, loving relationship. "Weekend Rach" was impishly craving some excitement and I did not want to deny myself that. I thought, *I am twenty-three. I have not been single since I was twenty, and I am bored of the good guys (for now).* Boy did I throw myself a bone. Now, I am smart enough to never put myself in actual danger, and don't you worry your pretty little mind, I did take this up with my therapist before jumping headfirst into shark-inhabited waters. She agreed that it was time to put "Nine-to-Five Rach" on the shelf for a moment and make a few mistakes. Humblebrag: I do want to further emphasize that I am levelheaded enough to not under any condition get myself into a situation that would actually negatively impact my life in the long run, so be careful out there, you crazy kids, and inquire with your therapist before playing with fire. Sexy, sexy fire.

Looking back on my encounters with my Adrenaline Guy, I have hashtag no regrets, but I do approach my time in-between hits with caution. He would get me high with his soft, bearded kisses and his sweet compliments that struck like electricity to the soul coming from his deep, sensual voice. My heart still races at the thought of his hands in my hair in my candlelit bedroom. These encounters were beyond intoxicating, but then, hours after he left, I would crash into a low, sometimes depressive place. I sought my next fix like a junkie. My therapist explained that this was a natural side effect because my body erupted with so many addictive chemicals when he was around.

Where I find balance now is in ensuring that I continue to live my life for me, not for my drug. I vow to never return to the self-sabotaging habits I practiced for a few months when Adrenaline Guy and I were at our peak. Some of these detrimental practices included stalking him on Instagram to see what he was up to, also online stalking a woman I thought he might potentially be romantic with, and I am not joking when I tell you guys I slept with my phone's sound on full blast every night for months, just in case he booty called me. I remember waking up in the morning after numerous restless nights only to have my day ruined the instant I checked my phone and saw that he had not texted me. Yikes, this is why self-help books exist, you guys.

When I first met this man, I was so transfixed by his presence that I was slightly out of tune with myself. After the waters leveled out and I returned to homeostasis, I was able to recognize this and proceed forward with caution. Now, I am not perfect, and you should all do as I say, not necessarily as I do. I am only human. I will admit I still see Adrenaline Guy every now and again. It has helped me to open my eyes to what exactly his effect on me is so it is no longer such a reckless and potentially dangerous indulgence.

Knowing the information I do now, I try to incorporate balance by maybe allowing myself a hit of my drug every once and a while. But now I am able to anticipate the withdrawal symptoms and plan accordingly by preparing myself for this guy to probably not text me every day of his life or ask me to be his wife. It is invigorating to be in the presence of a man so powerful because it is a precise test of my ability to remain genuine to myself and tap into my desires. I dabble in my drug but always take care to ensure I breathe, slow down, and do not forfeit myself in the process.

Ah yes, the time has inevitably arrived. This brings me to the topic of my biggest fault that I bring into relationships, especially romantic ones. HOT, right?! Who wants to date me? Don't all jump at once! Let's get into it. I fell in love for the first time when I was fifteen years old. He was a year older, tall with brown hair—hmm, as I am writing this, I am realizing that fifteen-year-old Rach was more aligned with her desires than I originally gave her credit for! Anyway, he was the cool bad boy who had a kind heart deep down. In high school, he was adored by everyone around him; his presence took up an entire room. He ran the show. We did what he wanted: rode around in his gray Mazda SUV, listened to his music, and played by his rules.

I loved every minute of it. I was just so thrilled to be in love. That sensation was so novel and momentous that it did not really matter to me when I would hear rumors about him telling classmates he was "only with me for the sex" or stories that were definitely true about him bragging to friends about sexual advances. I loved him, and I was confident that he loved me too despite his shitty behavior. A part of me was aware he did talk a big game, but I knew who he was behind closed doors and I was convinced all that talk was just for show.

Despite the love he expressed for me when no one else was around, he eventually had sex with another girl at a house party a year into our relationship. Months later, he found himself crying in my arms, begging me not to leave. Cheating aside, my instincts were correct because it turned out that deep down, he truly did not want to lose me. I bring this up because as I previously mentioned, I am addicted to feelings.

I get so wrapped up in the dopamine rush of attraction that I will disregard what is right for me. So, young and unaware of what I even wanted, I followed the lead of my guy, trusting that he knew the way. There was no yin to this yang happening here. Without balancing our desires with those of our partners, we become completely lost. I did not set boundaries on the behavior of my first love because I did not prioritize my own feelings, only his. When two people come together carrying their separate, complicated worlds to create a new, even more complicated world, an equilibrium must be developed and maintained.

Following my first, it was not long before I found someone else to get my love chemicals from. I spent my next few relationships morphing into whatever my person of interest wanted. I also became intensely insecure, associating every guy's night out with cheating because that was what happened to me the first time. I so desperately wanted a man to love me the way that I loved him, and I feared and anticipated his disloyalty as if it would inevitably happen, and if it did, it would be the end of all humanity. I had a boyfriend for a few years who turned out to love me in the same tenaciously possessive way that I loved him. We held an aggressively tight grip around each other because we did not know any better. I speculated that this guy was the one because I had finally gotten what I wanted! But the dynamic was far from balanced. He would accuse me of having another boyfriend at my college and I would yell at him for liking other girls' photographs online. Every time one of us went out to parties with friends, there was a dramatic blowout fueled by jealousy. I had no concept of what mutual emotional abuse was at the age of eighteen.

Towards the end of that relationship, I was growing up and finally beginning to learn how to tune into what *I* wanted, which was out. This was groundbreaking for me. I felt crippling, unmatched guilt for breaking this man's heart, but I reaped the rewards almost immediately. I felt empowered because I was finally able to control and care for my own experience rather than that of my significant other. My instinct has always been to put others first. I often worry about how my romantic partner is experiencing me significantly more than I worry about how I am experiencing him. It is not the most shockingly evil quality in the world, but when you are two years deep into a relationship and you discover that you have zero boundaries and do not know the first thing about who you are because you lack the ability to balance what you want with what they want, you run into problems.

I remember asking my most recent boyfriend, Tyler, what he thought of me at the end of our first date. We were in the foyer of the first apartment I had ever lived in. I remember putting my arms around his waist, connecting them in the back, creating a circle that encapsulated him in my embrace. We were flirting, kissing goodbye, and overall being hella cute. "So, what did you think? You gonna text me tomorrow? What's good, do you like me?" I teased.

He flashed his pearly white smile along with a laugh. "Mmmm, seven out of ten," he teased back, both of us understanding how into each other we had quickly become.

At the time, I thought I was being bold and transparent, avoiding any mind games about whether or not we were on the same page. That may be true, but in hindsight I can also now identify how deeply I craved his approval. I consider my relationship with Tyler to have been my first adult partnership. With him, I became educated about what it meant to be in a healthy relationship, made up of two equal parts. This man taught me to prioritize myself and my needs, but I still was not able to fully succeed in doing so. As a result of my history and my shortcomings in the self-awareness department, I still found myself bending in ways he did not even ask me to in a desperate attempt to make his life better and ultimately prevent him from ever wanting to break off the relationship. I altered my vision of my career and my future so that it would include him. I am going to mention one more time that he never even subtly hinted that he wanted me to do this. I was slowly losing myself without either of us really noticing.

Have you ever done something like this, sweet reader? Imbalance in a relationship can look different for everyone. For me, it means turning a blind eye to my sense of self. For you, it could show up as spending all of your time and money to visit someone who would not even get on the 101 for you. Disproportion in your relationship could mean forcing your partner to hang out with your friends every weekend and never asking if he or she would like to hang out with his or her friends. Regardless, I urge you to see yourself and your partner as whole entities, watering all of the plants of a relationship, not just the fragrant, sexy roses.

Of course, when you are in a relationship, you need to make sacrifices and compromises, but I was so young, and I would hit dangerous territory when I was in love. There was a part of me that believed if I illustrated the perfect life for my man by being the perfect girlfriend, he would never leave me for someone else. Obviously, I now know that this attempt does nothing but throw my life off-kilter and no matter what I do, I cannot control what is going on in the head of the one I love. I have learned that the best thing you can do for you and your partner is to be true to yourself and to love them gently, and hold them in your hand with an open palm, not a closed fist. Seeking the balance between prioritizing the needs of oneself and those of another is something I have struggled with time and time and again, but I can assure you it is a war worth fighting. Gear up, lovers!

My advice to anyone who suffers from a similar codependence issue is to take a step back and examine what you want out of life. It is most neutral and unbiased to do this while single, but, of course, if you are in a serious relationship it is extremely responsible to know what you and *only you* require and wish for. Make a list. Yeah, I said it. Make a damn list. Write down at least five marvelous qualities that you, independent of your partner, bring to a relationship. Make another damn list, or better yet write a damn book about what you want out of life (again, independent of your partner). Spend some time alone. Learn to treasure all of the remarkable, unique things about yourself. Personally, I have been doing so much of this lately that I authentically believe, to my core, that y'all are missing out BIG TIME by not being married to me, thank you very much. I am so serious, dude. I want you to get on my level of self-certainty. This way, when Adrenaline Guy does not text you back, you know who the real loser is in that situation. Spoiler alert, it's him.

At a young age, the undeniable fact that any guy I was dating was always going to be attracted to other women used to disturb me. I strained, starved, poked, and lasered myself to be the hottest thing ever so that they would—please, God, nooo—not cheat on me! I found freedom from this concept recently by again loosening my shackles and taking a moment to relax and reflect. In her book *Moody Bitches*, Julie Holland does an exquisite job of illustrating the neurology behind sex and attraction. I urge you to go and take a look. But not now, please, no! Do not abandon me! I learned that it is natural to be sexually curious outside of your committed relationship. How you choose to act on that is up to you and your partner, but perhaps just accepting that truth will be enough to set you free the way it did for me.

No longer was there pressure to be the most smoking hot, sexiest girlfriend ever, while also being the advice-giving therapist; the cute wifey cook; the lively adventure buddy; the most reliable dog co-parent; the adorable partner your parents would go gaga for; and so on. All I am saying is, I have to be all that *and* be your personal stripper? No thanks! That is too many hats for anyone to wear at one time. I do not care *who* you are. Emily Blunt, I am looking at you, you annoyingly perfect woman. But the truth is, we are all human. Treat yourself as such. Treat your partner as such. Have open, judgment-free conversations. The more you can both be honest about what your desires are, the more authentic you will both be, and in the end, you will not lose yourself in love the way yours truly always did.

Okay, back to adrenaline. I have a dramatic personality and I definitely catastrophize situations. I know this about myself. When something knocks me off my day-to-day agenda, and I have to adapt, I do it so quickly you will not even know what happened. For example, on Wednesday I got the news that I was going to have to find a new place to live. It is now Friday and I am officially on a lease for a new apartment. Oh, this does not sound crazy to you? You clearly do not live in Los Angeles then. This entire week I have been in a fog of adrenaline, frantically calling landlords, filling out applications, and driving around town like a madwoman. Or maybe just like a pack leader securing the safety and comfort of my dog and I. Did I mention I had the flu while doing all of this? I even already have Craigslist ads posted of all the junk from my current place that I am selling. It is probable that there is a less neurotic way to go about my productive manic streaks, but I have a nearly impossible time finding it.

Another example of this behavior is me currently writing twenty pages of this damn book in one day without taking a breath. When there is a task looming over my head, my body prioritizes checking it off the list as soon as possible and I will not rest until said task is completed. Moving into a new apartment over a couple days? Oh hell no, I will not sleep until every last one of my pieces of Ikea furniture is built and in place. I'm not going to lie, this addictive adrenaline high seems to have served me well. I do in fact get shit done, but I feel crazy, anxious, and uneasy while getting aforementioned shit done. Maybe there is some balance I can find somewhere so I do not end up feeling so drained at the end of it all. This is a part of the book where if you relate, I honestly do not have any suggestions yet. I am still not even fully convinced that this is a problem that needs fixing. Maybe you can email me some advice? Help ya girl out for once this time. God, I am sick of doing everything!

As artists, we often get trapped in the mindset that we must be doing anything and everything to advance our career at all hours of every day. "Nine-to-Five Rach" hustles all week long, taking dance classes, working out, attending auditions, and working gigs nonstop so I can afford my ever-climbing rent. This is all tremendous and important, but "Nine-to-Five Rach" has an impossible time leaving room for "Weekend Rach." Oftentimes, I will work myself to the bone with no day off for two months straight and then wonder why I end up with a sprained ankle or the flu. I am going to be blunt because I love you babes: "Nine-to-Five Rach" is a bitch. She is a drill sergeant, so rigid and strict in her actions that she may as well be a goddamn, no fun, party killin', cock-blockin' robot. When I do finally grow ill and take the time to rest, I feel immense guilt. Worry that I will never be successful creeps into my mind as I sit in a room at urgent care to get my concussion checked, wondering why the hell they thought Marvin Gaye's "Let's Get It On" would be a practical addition to their playlist.

In my experience, I have learned that we must not forget we are human beings before anything else. Without human experience, we cannot create art. I need to get better about allowing myself to rest and go out and spend time with friends. If I never took the time to go on any dates, I would have lost half the content in this book! I need to get better about recognizing my own emotions while spending time with romantic love interests. We try to stuff the sensitive, burned-out, creative human being that lives inside of us away into a tiny robot box. Then we ignore its knocks and cries for nourishment. Seriously, if you need this reminder as much as I do, take it—tattoo it on your forehead, scream it off a mountaintop, whatever you need to do. Just do not forget that life is about balance. Please *do not* forget to be a damn person!

And when you do take that time, please, for the love of cheesecake, do not feel fucking guilty about it! Okay, so I have not yet checked all the career goals off my list that I would like to, but what about all the dope things I have discovered about my psyche over the past few months? What about all the neat facts I learned in that book I read about hormones? And what about that amazing chocolate fondue I had and that cute blue-eyed boy I made out with? What about all the creative anecdotes I thought up in my head? Those matter.

To help myself remember this concept, I tattooed it on my forehead and I also made a list of vows. You should do the same. Envision practices you may be punishing yourself with for overindulging. Or maybe you are the opposite of myself and you party too much, only eat doughnuts, and need to focus more on work and squash! It works either way.

Here is mine:

I will get enough sleep, but I will also stay up late.

I will eat kale, but I will also eat chocolate … And cheese!

I will drink maca powder in my smoothies, but I will also drink wine.

I will exercise, but I will also rest.

I will clean my room, but I will also make a mess.

I will take alone time, but I will also be with friends.

(*Isolation is one of my fave punishments, hehe.*)

I will take dance classes and audition, but I will also feed my art with life.

I will value my independence, but I will also let people in.

I will walk my dog, but I will sing out loud to music while doing so.

I will budget, but I will also spend.

I will think critically, but I will also appreciate.

(*a.k.a. get the stick out of my ass*)

I will plan, but I will also live in the moment.

I will take care of others, but I will also take care of myself.

Now, you may notice that the tasks on the left-hand side of the list are chores, and sometimes punishments I engage in for allowing myself to do whatever is on the right side. The beginning of each sentence is a "Nine-to-Five Rach" task, whereas the end of each sentence is a "Weekend Rach" activity.

I read this list to my therapist because I told her I wanted to work on balance and she had me replace all the instances I used the word "but" in the sentences with the word "and."

Here is the result:

I will get enough sleep and I will also stay up late.

I will eat kale and I will also eat chocolate … And cheese!

I will drink maca powder in my smoothies and I will also drink wine.

I will exercise and I will also rest.

I will clean my room and I will also make a mess.

I will take alone time and I will also be with friends.

I will take dance classes and audition and I will also feed my art with life.

I will value my independence and I will also let people in.

I will walk my dog and I'll sing out loud to music while doing so.

I will budget and I will also spend.

I will think critically and I will also appreciate.

I will plan and I will also live in the moment.

I will take care of others and I will also take care of myself.

Her version looks more like a gentle, sweet lifestyle plan of action than my original, somewhat aggressive checklist, doesn't it? Dang, that lady sure knows what she is talking about. Now, if you would excuse me, I have been writing for twelve hours straight and should probably text that cute blue-eyed boy back to see if he wants to hang out tonight.

My Balance Vows

I will _____ and I will _____.

I will _____ and I will _____.

I will _____ and I will _____.

I will _____ and I will _____.

I will _____ and I will _____.

I will _____ and I will _____.

I will _____ and I will _____.

I will _____ and I will _____.

I will _____ and I will _____.

I will _____ and I will _____.

I will _____ and I will _____.

I will _____ and I will _____.

I will _____ and I will _____.

… 'til death do us part!

Chapter Two

Home is Where Your Ex's Sweatshirts Are

Because I have a phobia of criticism and disappointing people, I need to preface this chapter with a few key points. I had a lovely childhood and my parents are two of the best people that exist in this world. They work selfless careers to aid those in need and have given my brother and I love, care, attention, and pretty much worked their asses off their entire lives in order for us to succeed. There are days when receiving the unconditional love they give is challenging for me because I rarely have anything to offer in exchange. I feel an overwhelming sense of shame when they offer to fly across the country just to see me or send me money to cover an unanticipated medical expense required by my dog even though she is *my* responsibility, gosh. On top of passing on what I consider to be stellar genes, they taught me to prioritize happiness over money and that helping others came before helping myself. We should establish a code word for me to drop every time I start crying while writing because YUP. GET ME A TISSUE.

Receiving unconditional love is a tricky idea for most humans to grasp. Adopting a dog actually enabled me to comprehend this concept because I began to embody the notion of doing anything and everything for another being without expecting anything in return. The people who first taught me how it feels to be loved no matter what, my parents, are the absolute greatest, most kindhearted people I know. They also happened to create the third-greatest person I know, my brother, so obviously they did a damn good job. But I cannot fully reflect on who I am without tracing back to my upbringing. It is Psychology 101, you guys! I am a functioning member of society, healthy, and I like to think I bring joy to others as a result of them going above and beyond their duty as parents. Any mental struggle I may face because of their mental struggles is solely my responsibility now that I am an adult.

As children, however, their circumstances were far more difficult than mine, and they are human, so by default, their insecurities are my insecurities and their shortcomings are my shortcomings. Fault belongs to no one here. Nobody is perfect, and they did the best they could. And that is all we can ask of anyone.

About Mom

I have a surpassingly special relationship with my mother. Growing up, she never failed to be there for a hug, a batch of cookies, or reading time. Just give me the whole box of tissues—it is going to be a long one. When I summon childhood memories of my mother, warmth and a sense of comfort encompass my body. I can detect her aura of love that she carried around my brother and me, her eyes unfailingly on us and our needs, never in the mirror on her own. I have so many bright and sunshiny memories of my childhood; I am privileged to have experienced it as a happy time of life, rid of the burdens of the real world.

My mother and I are both driven by emotion and feelings, which resulted in some conflict during my hormonal teenage years. There were a lot of hypercharged altercations like "WTF, Mom? I am FIFTEEN! Why can't I spend the night at my boyfriend's?!" And "UGH, you really have to call this party to make sure the parents are there?! SO embarrassing!" In present days, we both express remorse regarding how we handled some situations amid those years and luckily, we can laugh on it now. In adulthood, my relationship with my mother has evolved into a friendship filled with mutual support and long talks about life during car rides when it is just the two of us.

Somewhere along the line, probably once I surpassed my mom in height, and in later years when she lost a lot of the youthful muscle I remember her having in my childhood, I developed the staggering instinct to protect her. What from, I am not exactly sure. She is about five feet tall. I stand at the adorable national average of five foot four. She carries a tiny frame, is in her fifties, and has developed osteoporosis. So when I hug her, I feel her adorably petite, bony shoulders in my embrace. As I mentioned before, she is emotional. When we get together you can find us both blubbering away at old photographs or to a sad song or tearfully singing along to a *Mamma Mia* movie. It is a mess, and at times, too much to handle. Due to my own stubbornness and avoidance behaviors, I have learned to dodge scenarios that stir up a lot of emotions for both of us. When my mom cries, I start to feel panic, immediately wanting it to stop and for her to feel better. This is probably true for anyone who has a mother who they love. To this day I still feel the desire to be a backbone for her even though she is a grown woman and rationally, I am aware that she does not need it.

My mother experienced her own parents' divorce when she was at a vulnerable age, around ten or eleven. I am no doctor, but I do know that if a child witnesses parents fighting, separating, and/or leading overall unsatisfactory love lives under a shared roof, that young mind is altered. Divorce has thus shaped the psychology of millions of people. I gather that my mother's parents' divorce had some influence on the way she sees love. My grandparents' generation prioritized family and placed the worth of a woman on the man she married. My mother's father egged her on at a young age with questions like, "So you have a boyfriend yet?" There are obvious reasons that this is damaging. I am so grateful to live in a time when women are asked about their careers and not just "Hey, when are you planning to have a baby?! Time is a-ticking." Of course, there is still way too much of that going around, but I am optimistic that we will get there, people!

In a recent FaceTime call with my maternal grandmother, she became tearful discussing the topic of love and relationships. Through sobs, she begged me to please "wait for a good man" and declared, "All I pray for is for you to have a great husband." Now, that conversation made me sick, but akin to my mom, my grandmother is a wonderful soul who is also doing her very best with the bridge cards she has been dealt. She is eighty-seven, from the South, and got married for the first time on her eighteenth birthday, so we can all cut her some slack. I understand the desire of parents or grandparents for their offspring to find love. It is a beautiful, godly feeling. It is *the* feeling.

Feelings, feelings, feelings! I wish I could explain to my grandmother not to worry because I have in fact experienced that incredible sensation of true love and devotion with a partner and just because I am not with him right now does not mean I am doomed forever. I was also tempted to explain to her that, "GRANDMA, listen! Like most girls my age, I have an Instagram account *full* of direct messages from self-proclaimed perfect suitors offering to be my husband. I am not worried, Grandma. I am alone by active choice because it is presently more beneficial to my well-being to fly solo than to be in a relationship when I do not yet have the tools to prioritize myself. And not for nothing, but no one is leaving my toilet seat up, causing me to fall in first thing in the morning, thank you very much!" What my grandmother intrinsically wants is for me to be happy, and thankfully we have a mutual understanding that even if my happiness does not look the way she conceives it should (wedded to a noble prince at age twenty-three), I will do everything I can to build a life of joy and fulfillment for myself.

Now that we know a little bit more about my mom's developmental psychology, we can better understand her and in turn better understand my developmental psychology, and finally, better understand me! Yay! In conversations with my mom, we have uncovered our countless similarities. Like so many of us, my mother had some natural insecurities and worries around dating. Similar to me, she has admitted herself into therapy to better her ability to accept love and feel emotionally safe and trusting in romantic relationships. From what she has expressed to me, I gather that a number of her self-doubts in relationships are similar to struggles I face. Thanks a lot, grandparents! I told you getting married at eighteen was a bad idea, Grandma!

My mother also struggles with restrictive eating behaviors and the body insecurity that I, and so many of us do. Hanging out in the nursery at the local gym was a regular part of my childhood and I watched my mother run in races and cheered her on from the sidelines. These can potentially be perfectly healthy activities for families, but looking back through my childhood lens, it is difficult for me to determine whether or not my mother had a healthy relationship with exercising. This is related to my narrative because watching my mom workout was part of my conditioning. Again, I cannot attest to her experience, but in more recent years when I have been transparent about my struggles with food and eating, my mom has opened up to me about hers as well. She has put forth an extreme amount of effort to maintain her figure over the course of my life. I grew up watching her diet and skip dessert. Raising a child to have a healthy relationship with food is damn near impossible in my opinion. It is such sketchy territory for so many of us.

On the other hand, my father lives his best life with food. My mom never fails to have a supply of homemade chocolate chip cookies for him so he can engage in his nightly cap of those and a tall glass of milk. Because my dad does not see food as the enemy, he loves to make self-deprecating jokes when he eats massive quantities. After a hefty meal, one of his favorite lines is "hmmm, can't understand why I haven't lost any weight." Overeating does not give him the anxiety that it blesses the rest of us with, so he is able to have a grand old time and not think twice about it.

My mom has confided in me that she has felt worried about what others might think if they notice her practicing restrictive eating behaviors. In one instance she completely cut out sweets and politely declined dessert at a party (something that we codependent dieters already feel so ashamed of), only to have my dad chime in, "Wow, isn't it great? She is cutting out sweets. I could never!", shedding more light on the situation, and embarrassing my already self-conscious mother. I do not bring this up to shame my father. I admire his partnership with his body and with food and wish so badly that I had inherited his and not my mother's. It is evident that he does not contemplate these gags and their effects because, of course, if he knew, he would never discuss food in that manner.

A couple years ago, I informed my mom that when Dad jokes about walking to get the mail because he needs to exercise off the Thanksgiving dinner we just ate, it makes me feel even worse about the meal. Since that confrontation with my mom, I have not heard a peep about food or exercise from my dad. He was probably consumed with the guilt (because, hi! Yes, we are a family of self-blamers) of possibly harming her, my brother, and myself with his thoughtless antics. He advanced in the most heroic way possible; he gracefully and silently eliminated the problem. Bless him. Growing up with a mother who did not love her body and experienced her relationship with food as a challenge definitely contributed to the development of my restrictive eating disorder; that is just the truth. It is no one's fault, so Mom, if you are reading this, you will STOP that guilt RIGHT NOW, please. It is just the way the fattening cookie crumbles.

My brother is a runner who has also struggled with his fair share of self-deprivation. I recall a depressing phase when I would often bake something yummy and he would politely decline. I was still in high school, but when he moved away to his nearby college, I watched him abruptly become troublingly thin. It is heartbreaking to see someone you love go through this. I am not fully cognizant of all the details because so often in families we shield our pain from those closest to us. I have certainly done my fair share of masking my struggles to avoid the discomfort of confrontation and to save my family from worry. From what I could see and from what my mother told me, my brother intentionally dropped a concerning amount of weight when he went off to his freshman year of college. Just like me. Luckily, he was able to receive treatment and he seems to be doing much better in more recent years. He would not be my big bro without his unmatched adoration for Chipotle and pizza.

More about Dad

If you have audibly giggled at any point while reading this book, you have my father to thank for that. While deeply intuitive, he sees the world through a sunny lens, never taking himself or any predicament life throws at him too seriously. When the environment that surrounds me appears chaotic, he is calm. When life around me seems increasingly sad, he makes me laugh. I find myself taking on his role in numerous situations.

Last year, I surprised my mother with a girls' trip up to Montreal for a couple days before Christmas. We drove up there as it is about a five-hour drive from my hometown. We parked her car outside the Airbnb in the icy cold while we waltzed the streets of Montreal all weekend and hopped on and off the nearby metro. When the time came to venture back home, we attempted to start the car only to discover the battery had died. Somehow one of the overhead lights had been bumped on, causing the helpless Kia Sportage to die in the frigid temperatures while my mother and I had indulgently enjoyed ourselves over cappuccinos and croissants.

My mom's initial reaction was panic. She began to catastrophize, which I am often a fan of doing too. When I face a disruption or disturbance, oftentimes I urgently stress about the worst possible outcome. It is likely this trait showed up in my personality because it is one my mother also has. But in this instance, because she was immediately struck with worry, the pack leader in me calmly began to problem solve. *Okay,* I thought. *It is all good in the hood. We just need to find someone to jump the car, then we will proceed from there.* Of course it crossed my mind that it was ten degrees outside, we were now locked out of our Airbnb, and in a foreign country with no access to our AAA service. But in that moment, I was my father's daughter. "You cannot worry about the ninth hole when you are still on the eighth," my dad always says.

I left my mom with the car and began jogging around the icy cross streets, asking strangers if they had jumper cables and/or a moment to help us out. I got quite a few nos. Okay, keep looking. I stumbled upon a young man sitting in his warming-up car, likely about to take off to go to work. Through fogged-up windows, I asked if he could help us and sure enough, he could. He was the kindest man ever, with a sweet French accent, and insisted it was no burden at all. He knew his way around the mechanics of the car and soon we were on our way quicker than we could say "merci beaucoup" to this gentleman fifteen times over. Sort of a low-stakes, anticlimactic story for you (we have all had a dead car battery before), but I like it because I have never felt more like my father than I did in that moment. I did everything as he would have, which was exactly what my mother and I needed.

My father is a simple man with a lot of love for his family, golf, and chocolate cake. It does not take much to make him happy because he grew up with so little. His goofy sense of humor is a hit among his coworkers and friends of our family. I am so grateful that I grew up learning how to incorporate humor and lightheartedness into my daily life. It is a quality more healing to me than I can currently explain.

Both of my parents work as therapists in a chemical dependency unit of a health-care system in their town. They labor for the people who need it most; a number of their clients forced to see them by court order. In my opinion, talking to drug addicts about their problems is not the best aphrodisiac, but I guess it was for my parents because they met at a job in the eighties and still work together to this day.

My father is a recovering alcoholic and has been sober for thirty-three years. His own experience likely fuels his life's work but other than that, he does not speak of it to family or friends. He was newly sober when he courted my mother. We have all been so fortunate of his strength so as to not to have to bear the consequences of an active addiction. I cannot even begin to wrap my mind around how difficult battling alcoholism is. He chose to break a family pattern and create a better life for himself and for that, I regard him with the highest respect, but his alcoholism was almost never mentioned in our household. I do not remember when I learned of it—it just seemed like a known fact that no one ever mentioned. My mother was open about it, even announcing with pride the day my dad hit twenty-five years of sobriety. We congratulated him, but that was the extent of the discussion. It was as if someone got a really terrible haircut but like, way more serious, obviously. Everyone was thinking about it, but no one was talking about it. I respect his decision to not bring it up throughout our childhood because it is so crucial for children to feel trusting of and safe with their guardians.

My father is and always has been the most reliable person I know. Now that I am older and gazing inward at my own qualities, I wonder how I would be different if my father had displayed some vulnerability and opened up about his sobriety once my brother and I were at a safe age to handle it. I cannot help but acknowledge the fact that my dad's silence on the matter consequently conditioned my brother and me to believe that the darkest parts of ourselves were meant to be left unacknowledged. Our truest, deepest, ugliest flaws were to stay hidden in order to protect those we love. Aha moment! This belief is so heavily ingrained in my blood and has manifested itself in my personality in so many ways.

I find myself drawn to men who are going through emotional turmoil because I feel as though I can aid them through it. My father never really opened up to us about his feelings, so I hunt for any opportunity to pull out emotions from my male romantic partners as a way to fill that void. What my father withheld from my brother and me in the emotional vulnerability department, my mother overcompensated for. I do remember getting attention from my dad in the form of quality time, playtime, hugs and kisses, and the verbal affirmation "I love you" that is so essential for kids to hear growing up.

Although he is still very reserved about his personal problems, in his older age, I have witnessed my dad soften and have seen his emotions emerge in ways I never did growing up. I gather that I am drawn to men who are slightly closed off emotionally because it is what I am used to and if I can pry them open it will be a win of an old childhood battle for me. I know "daddy issues" is so cliché and boring, and I do not consider myself to have them because I do have such a wonderful father, but we do all face the consequences of our parents' pitfalls, no matter how minor or well-intentioned.

I never considered myself to be the child of an alcoholic because my dad has been sober my whole life, but listening to a book that discusses addiction and its effects on relationships (*Women Who Love Too Much* by Robin Norwood) opened my eyes to the fact that my father's addiction affected me growing up. I am more genetically predisposed to addiction, and from what I have witnessed, that addiction has not manifested itself in drugs or alcohol, thank God, but more so in my addiction to love and relationships and all of the lovely chemicals that come along with them. We can work with this one! I am so thankful every day that I never had the opportunity to play with hard drugs while dangerously young because who knows where

I would have ended up. "Helping" impossible men open up has caused me to turn a blind eye to my own issues. Likely due to the fact that I grew up in the home of a recovering alcoholic, I became codependent, especially in romantic relationships. I am currently attempting to treat this condition, working hard every day to look inward at myself and try not to control the mind of my man. Dismissing my obsessive thought patterns (without judgment) regarding men has been an extreme challenge for me, but I am determined to do so. My health depends on it.

I sure am no professional here. If you were to ask me the definition of codependency, I am not confident I would be able to settle on one specific, descriptive universal diagnosis despite having read multiple books on the condition. If you asked me what codependency is, however, I would be able to identify a particular and definite feeling. For me, codependency is the complete mental exhaustion I feel while concerning myself with the experiences of others. It is the pit I get in my stomach as I drive my friends to the beach I wanted to go to and we hit traffic, extending the ride. I do not mind the extra fifteen minutes of sitting in the car, but I worry my friends will. It is the crippling self-blame I feel when those around me behave in a negative way. It is the frantic, sweaty search for a fault in myself in order to justify a man's rejection of me. It is that uncontrollable urge to blurt out the words "you should go to therapy" to my boyfriend every day I am with him. It is the shaky, blurry, lost sense of identity that often emerges when I am in long-term romantic relationships. It is the worry and the stressful thoughts concerning others and how I can help them that keep me up at night.

Codependency may look like this to you or it may look completely different. It could be a pattern you experience of dating abusers, manipulators, or addicts. It could be working so hard to assist the depressed friend in your life that your mental health begins to decline as a result. It could be waiting until you have company over to light your favorite candle. It could be an extremely low bank account balance because you are too afraid to ask friends to pay you back for all those times you spotted them. I think our culture romanticizes this concept too much. I see garbage on the internet in the form of sad tweets reading something like "use your healing soul, people need you" or "I love broken ones, then I become the broken one, wahh." Let's be done with all this toxic shit! Determined to free myself from this crippling condition, I try to keep this mantra in my mind: "He is responsible for himself." It is a constant reminder to myself that the adults around me are exactly that. Adults. And I cannot control their well-being no matter how hard I try. This mantra has helped me begin to detach my overwhelming emotional involvement. I love this quote I found in *Codependent No More* by Melody Beattie:

> "It (detachment) is not detaching from the person whom we care about, but from the agony of involvement." – Al-Anon Member

"I'm fine!!!!" is a statement often leaving my lips when I am around my parents. Having therapist parents results in seemingly endless unwarranted prying into my psyche when I am just trying to drink my coffee and eat my oatmeal; it is too fucking early for this, Mom! I remember when my parents would drive up to Buffalo while I was in college for a visit. Frantically, I would clean my apartment, dress in loose clothes to hide my weight loss, and prepare myself to greet them at the door with a smile no matter what had been stressing me out that day. I always wanted them to worry about me less than they did, so I assured them that school was good, I was eating enough, making time for friends, and was yes, very, very happy! It was so much simpler for me to just shield my parents from my inner struggles.

Recently I found myself talking to a new guy and realized I was continuously complaining to him about the physical pain I was experiencing. I have chronic migraines and they were making a hot comeback, so that was a subject of our discussion when he asked me how I was. I also found us talking about other physical issues I was encountering like acne, back pain, ankle sprains, you name it! What a nightmare. I still cannot believe I got a second date. My codependence instantly made me self-conscious, worrying that he would think I am a sensitive pain in the ass for whining about all my ailments. I am all right though, guy! I swore it was no big deal retracting and minimizing all of my previous complaints. Hello, patterns, nice to see you again.

It is uncanny the way our relationships with our parents translate into future romantic ones. Hey, Freud was onto something! Anyway, I began to look inward, as I do, and question why the hell I was so cool with posting all over my Instagram stories about my physical pain but any time there was emotional pain, I either made it a joke or avoided the subject completely. Today, I am cognizant that this is all due to the fact that I learned at a young age that showing emotional pain got me too much attention from my parents. It was a big, messy, complicated deal. When I had a knee scrape, it was a predictable, easy fix. Without fail, I got a kiss, some Neosporin, a Band-Aid, and sometimes if I was lucky, ice cream! What's up, positive reinforcement!? Physical pain was treatable, curable, and rewarded with sympathy, whereas emotional pain usually just led to more questions, hard work, and waterworks from everyone.

Nowadays, I often still avoid the subject of emotional turmoil when I can, but I learned that my parents are adults (what?) and they can handle it. They actually gain more satisfaction out of knowing and connecting to the real me than being lied to about the untrue notion that I am fine, I swear! This has brought me to a new level of comfort around my parents. I no longer feel the need to anxiously tiptoe through the house while home for the holidays or put up an exhausting front while worried about their worry. Of course, I still must withhold my wittiest jokes that contain sensitive material like dicks and suicide around them, but hey, some boundaries are a good thing.

More about Brother

Meanwhile, when I relocated to Los Angeles at the age of twenty-one to pursue a selfish dream in the arts, my brother packed his bags for law school. My brother is my favorite person to brag about, so here I go; I am not going to waste another moment. He runs marathons, a concept I still cannot wrap my mind around even after witnessing him achieve the task in person. He is currently in his third year at Georgetown Law and already has a job lined up for after graduation.

For some reason, my brother's intense academic success was never intimidating to me. My parents did a spectacular job of never making me feel as though I was less because I was not in triple-accelerated advanced-level everything in school. I applauded his accomplishments while chasing feelings and doing whatever the hell made me happy—the title of a true artist, I am proud to claim. My brother is on track to pursue his professional dream of becoming a public defender, a voice for people who need it the most, just like my parents. They are all so selfless, it is borderline annoying, right?!

My brother is also one of the funniest people I know. One of my favorite things he has ever said was while we were visiting one of my mother's friend's homes outside of Boston. The dogs were all over him. Happily accepting the love of the animals, my brother announced that whenever his friends ask him for advice on why doggos are so fond of him, he instructs them to simply take fewer showers. Amazing! I laughed for like three days. In that moment I recognized that he is one hundred percent related to me despite all the youthful teasing about me being from Mars.

My parents and my brother are all so kind, it is nearly irritating. Anyone who has met them would attest to that. A lot of people who have met me would also say that one of my dominant qualities is kindness as well. Those people should meet my family, seriously! I do not feel like an outcast around them, but I do at times feel as though my strong personality dominates the family. As a child and teenager, my drama would take the stage while the three of them did what they could to help me ride my waves of emotion with endless patience. I do have a strong personality, but they are all so chill, it makes me mad sometimes! I remember being home for a visit not too long ago. Everyone was at the house, but my mom was asking *me* what we should eat for dinner and when. It is likely because I am dramatic and less easygoing than them, so they do not want to upset me, but they frequently look to me for leadership. I replied to my mom with something like "there's other people here, ask them!" in a huff.

My dominance of my small family has formulated me to become an alpha female. I find that in my relationships with other women, I take lead. I like to be in control by making plans so I can come and go on my own terms. I am incredibly organized and particular about the way I want orders to play out. Micromanaging can also be a symptom of codependence.

Oftentimes, codependents deal with difficult people who do not change no matter how freaking hard we try, so we are left to desperately attempt to gain control by being Nazis about the vacation itinerary or something like that. My desire to do things my way sometimes causes me to butt heads with other alpha females. One of my best friends is even more of an alpha female than I am (she is an older sibling, an alpha in her romantic relationships, has a badass boss-bitch marketing job, etc.) so when we are in that group, I have learned to allow her to take the driver's seat.

Sometimes I feel uncomfortable in the role of alpha female because deep down it is not actually what I want. In certain situations, nothing would get done if I did not take action, so in those, I will. This is why I like to date alpha males. In my romantic relationships, I get to indulge in my submissiveness, my femininity, and chill out a little bit. It feels good. I like to be pursued by men who make the plans, know what they want, and challenge me to be a better person. I cannot be with a passive man because like I do with my family, I will take alpha and end up walking all over the guy, and I will *not* enjoy myself while doing it.

My ex, Tyler, was exactly what I needed. We ended on great terms and still have a lot of love for each other, so I feel comfortable talking about how perfectly compatible we are even now, for the sake of self-discovery. As I mentioned, having parents who enabled me to get away with too much resulted in my current requirement of someone who does not put up with my bullshit. Any time I had car problems, my dad would take the car, get it fixed, put air in the tires, and let me know when it was ready to drive again. When my tire pressure light was on in my car for the millionth time, I begged Tyler to please just handle it while I stayed in the car and scrolled through Twitter. Nope, he was not having it. It did not matter how cute I was;

he made me get out of the car and learn once and for all how to check my tire pressure and fill it up myself. Alpha move. As much as I protested in the moment, I secretly loved it.

Another example of how this dominant personality works well with me was once when we went fishing. After what seemed like hours of no excitement, my line got a bite. I reeled it in and had caught a decent-sized fish! On camping trips as a child, I fished with my family and when I made a catch, my dad would praise me and then proceed to unhook the fish and set it free. With Tyler, I squealed with the joy of my success and handed it to him to please unhook, "the poor little guy cannot breathe!" He looked me dead in the eye and told me I was going to do it. Excuse me, what? This fish is dying; I am so bad at this! I insisted he do it for the greater good of all animals. He would not budge. "You can do it," he said with undeniable certainty. Adrenaline surged through my veins as I attempted to wiggle the hook loose. I was full of remorse for this unlucky little fella. I wondered what he did in a past life to deserve to encounter such an incompetent fisherman like myself. I do not know what the proper term is for when this happens to a fishy, but the hook had double penetrated the poor guy, making it that much more difficult to free. I was able to get it partly unstuck but not all the way.

I pleaded with Tyler to please help, but he still would not. I was so mad as I continued to grapple with this hook. I was terrified as I watched the gills on the fish gasp for breath. By some miracle, eventually the hook gave way and I was able to release it fully. I threw the traumatized animal back in the water as soon as I could. I may never fish again, but Tyler was right, I could do it. He believed in me more than I believed in myself in various areas of my life and he was rigid enough to not allow me to sell myself short with laziness. I will always be grateful to him for that.

Because I just spent the last chapter giving my parents a hard time about their most personal vulnerabilities, I want to take a moment to express gratitude for some of the amazing traits they have passed on to me and not just these magical cheekbones! As noted, these people are to thank for my sense of humor, my empathy, my compassion for others, and my ability to feel so deeply. My parents are both painfully self-aware, always working hard to be better in every part of their lives. They continually strive to improve in their personal lives, their professional careers, and their hobbies—my dad with his golf game, and my mom with her singing and knitting. They are humble people who are loved by the world around them. I have witnessed their care for their own parents in their old age and handling of their deaths with grace and love. They have a lovely relationship with one another that I still do not fully understand because never in a million years would I want to work with my partner at my job. Growing up watching a loving, mutually supportive relationship undoubtedly paved the way for me to end up there eventually. All of the things I love about myself are the things I love about them.

No one is perfect and we all inherit faults in our childhoods. That is just the deal when being raised by humans. Both of my parents' childhoods contained numerous challenges and they have spent their lives rising above the tragic patterns they could have easily passed on to my brother and I. My parents made me intuitive enough to get to where I am today. I did not die of a drug overdose, influenced by a terrible boyfriend. I have stood face-to-face with and battled my eating disorder. I have worked tirelessly to make myself a successful, happy person. I confronted and have healed so many personal issues at a young age. I wrote a damn book at twenty-three, all because of the extraordinary woman my parents raised me to be. Thank you, Mom and Dad.

Chapter Three

Roasted Kale is a Pathetic Excuse for a Food

This is honestly the hardest topic for me to write about—no, not because it opens painful wounds, silly, we have been over this! I love anything and everything involving emotional trauma! Eating disorders are difficult for me to discuss because I still do not fully have a handle on my own. I feel as though I should not have the audacity to give advice on such a dangerous subject, so that is precisely not what I am going to do. I am going to share my experiences with you because from my vantage point, there are global unhealthy eating habits and trends that we do not speak regularly about enough. There are symptoms residing in so many of us that remain undiagnosed and untreated. I am going to share my experiences because we need to be open about the psychological presence eating disorders weigh on our lives. This chapter is more of a *let's hug it out, you are not alone* chapter rather than a *here are all the answers* chapter. As a matter of fact, that is how this entire book seems to be turning out, isn't it? Do not blame me; you are the one reading a book by a twenty-three-year-old.

If you have never struggled with body dysmorphia, an eating disorder, or even something as simple and common as low self-esteem, congratulations, I want to read your book! Seriously, mail me a copy. If that is your case, I worry this chapter (and entire book) may sound whiny and as though I am searching for pity. I can assure you I am not. I am a pro at throwing my own pity parties by myself in my bathtub, so I promise that sympathy is not what I seek from you. If you are pretty much any normal person on the planet, I have an inclination that you may be able to relate in some way.

I remember being about nine years old, hanging out with my friends in between our dance classes. We would run wild during our free time, through the foyer of the lobby and out on the sidewalk and back again. We would sing, dance, and laugh with so much energy, and only God knows where it came from considering we had already participated in hours of physical activity that day. I remember the exact spot in that old purple dance studio where I was standing when this conversation occurred. A classmate, possibly a year or two older than me, was casually pointing out how because she had skipped breakfast that morning before coming to dance, her tummy looked smaller in the mirror in her ballet leotard.

In another instance, I remember being away for summer camp at the ripe, insecure age of thirteen, fooling around with friends after dark. A group of guys kept laughing about their newest joke. A "Booty-Do!" they would erupt in hysterics, referencing miscellaneous females. What is a *Booty-Do* you ask? "It's when her stomach sticks out further than her BOOTY-DO!" they would all-too-proudly inform you, accompanied by more laughter.

There are countless examples of situations like these that shape people's ideas of what they want their body to look like. Of course, we mustn't forget about fitness magazines, Hollywood, the porn industry, and so on—the list of unattainable body standards goes so far on it is truly exhausting! I am not going to bore you with more examples of how society shames perfectly healthy, fed bellies, thighs, arms, ankles, necks, and jaws (sheesh) because I have faith that you can also conjure up numerous situations in your own experience when the world made you feel as though you would not be accepted if you did not fit a certain body type.

For me, I always wanted to be thin, and if I am being honest, I still do. Nevertheless, I grew up loving food. My mother is an amazing cook and baker. For her and for our family, eating together is special and a testament of love and quality time. It is safe to conclude that I had a pretty average, mostly healthy relationship with food growing up. With the exception of a few harsh influences of the dance world and the media, boy did I enjoy my food! I can still recall how it felt to sit in a sticky booth at the Roadhouse Grill, a restaurant near our house that we would venture to nearly every Tuesday to take advantage of their *kids eat free* special. It was one of those joints where you could throw your peanut shells on the floor.

After spiking our bodies with sodium from the peanuts, I would unfailingly order a root beer, chicken tenders, and fries (real original, I know). I cannot mention this place without recalling the pillows of warm heaven they would present almost immediately after you sat down. A basket of the whitest of white rolls and the creamiest of butter, seductively waiting to be lathered on with a steak knife for some reason; a pairing that created the most intense pleasure I had ever known prior to discovering vibrators many, many years later. I can remember being oh-so-present, enjoying every bite of my meal.

Sadly, this is a foreign feeling for me and for many adults now. On the occasion that I do indulge in something so delicious that it contains the God-blessed gift of gluten, and I allow butter anywhere near it, I will taste it, enjoy it for a moment, and then cut myself off *or* fall headfirst into an uncontrollable binge-like state. HUH? I want my money back, dude. How did I go from sitting crisscross applesauce on a yellow booth seat, yelling at my dad for stealing one of my French fries, to this seemingly never-ending cycle of cravings, guilt, and shame? Here is where I do not have all the answers and encourage anyone who is suffering from an unhealthy relationship with body image and/ or food to please consult a medical professional. I know I am probably funnier and cooler than them, but I am serious, honey. Get better. We need you.

When I was seventeen years old, I downloaded the MyFitnessPal app because I saw a popular social media influencer mention she used it to keep herself "in check" when she "needed" to "lose a few pounds." I knew what calories were, but I had never tracked or restricted prior to this detrimental app download. (I now like to call this app the MyEatingDisorderPal.) I entered all my statistics into the app and selected *Sure! Losing 1 lb. per week sounds perfect!* Without understanding how the app worked, I began tracking everything I ate every day and using it as a sick game to stay within the very low number (bare minimal for survival) of calories it recommended I consume.

Within months, I had lost a significant amount of weight without really even meaning to. I went away to college and came home for breaks to receive praise for how "great I looked" and was hounded with questions about my college body and "OMG. What is your workout routine?" I gladly drank in the attention, not knowing my body was in a state of starvation. I also was unaware of how dramatically small I had gotten until years later when I reflected back on photographs. In those days, I would step on a scale every morning. Again, I thought I looked fine; I was happy to be skinny, but watching the numbers on the scale drop day after day was the most intoxicating bit.

People often talk about how eating disorders are more about control than anything else, and that concept was eagerly manifesting itself into my life with its tail wagging proudly behind it. I had just relocated to a new place, away from friends and family, and everything was challenging and complicated, but making numbers go down on a scale was simple and easy. It was predictable and it was pleasurable. I learned to isolate myself for meals by living in a dorm room with no regular friends to eat with. I would go downstairs to the dark, depressing dining hall and get egg whites for dinner if I only had one hundred calories "left" in MyFitnessPal for that day and then bring them back up into my room and eat them alone. No one was around to tell me egg whites were not a dinner. No one was around to pay attention when I would disappear to the gym and do hours of cardio if I had exceeded my daily allowance. On tired, sore legs, I would walk back to my room, exhausted by life.

An evening of my sophomore year of college is seared into my memory and to this day, I place myself there when I need a reminder of the dark places this illness has the power to take me. I love spending time with my friends, and I love cooking, baking, and eating with them. It had been one of those nights I adored so much. Chips, wine, TV, laughs—a wonderful pastime I required on the weekends to get me through my life at school. I do not recall exactly what happened in between leaving my friend's apartment and returning to mine, but I remember feeling overwhelming remorse regarding the snacks I had consumed. I was no stranger to this feeling of regret, but the next thing I knew, I was on my knees on the bathroom floor, violently wiggling my hand around the back of my throat, begging it all to come back up and out of my stomach. My heart was racing, and my skin was balmy with sweat. Not much expelled—my gag reflex is pretty much nonexistent (hey, boys!)—so I grew more vicious with myself, hoping so badly for a purge. I remember the feeling of shame after the fact and crying for the rest of the night.

The next morning, I explained what had unfolded to my boyfriend at the time and he warned me that if I were to ever do anything like that again, he would have to tell my parents. That was enough motivation for me at the time to refrain from any additional attempts to purge. Nowadays, the thought tempts my mind, but I bring myself back to that place, one of the darkest of my life, to prevent myself from ever inflicting that sort of aggression upon myself again. If it were physically easy for me to purge, I worry that I would be more drawn to it. Regardless, it is one of the most violent things someone can do to themselves. That night, I became gravely cognizant of this, so as a result I have been able to stay away since. If I ever feel the desire to purge after eating, I try to recall the shame and disappointment I had that night. Sometimes I am completely baffled that this world and our minds convince us that we need to commit such heinous acts upon our own bodies. I see that nineteen-year-old girl on the floor of her bathroom as the saddest and most ill I have ever been.

Unfortunately, to this day, some of the pernicious dieting habits I mentioned are still a part of my life. I have given up the hours of cardio and bland egg whites, *thank God*. I have been in therapy for years. I initially realized I needed help about three years after I began tracking my food and exercise while I was home for the holidays watching a video of my brother and me as kids. We were on summer vacation at a cottage we visited every year. I was about three or four years old in this tape and I had a cute little purple swimsuit on and we were gearing up to go to the pool. It sounds corny, but seeing that little blonde baby so comfortable in her skin, probably thinking about how much she loved cookies, brought me to tears. It was devastating for me to witness such a carefree spirit juxtaposed against my current restrictive, rigid self in the present day.

I began the three-step eating disorder program at my school—meetings with a nutritionist, psychotherapy, and a physical health evaluation. The nutritionist was a kind older woman who was patient with my stubborn ways about caloric intake and attempted to convince me that my body needed more. She gave me suggestions for some healthy ways I could add more nutrients into my diet. The therapist helped me tackle certain emotional issues and confront the fact that I was hurting a part of myself by engaging in these restrictive behaviors. Ultimately, however, the most harrowing piece of this program for me was the physical examination. On paper, I was a "healthy weight" for my height despite eating so few calories every day. My bones were not protruding, and I was not white in the face (well, not any whiter in the face than anyone would anticipate from living in the tundra that is Buffalo, New York). I did not even have abs, dammit! I was not anemic, and my blood tests did not result as those of someone who was malnourished. My skin was healthy, my hair was long, and I appeared to be doing very well. Glowing even!

This is the tricky thing about eating disorders that I have found—they are a disease of the mind that sometimes reveal themselves in visible ways but oftentimes, they do not. I feel very fortunate that my eating disorder has never caused any serious, dangerous physical health problems for me. I am acutely aware that this is not the case for everyone—again, please see a doctor, my love, if you are struggling. Even if you are not sure if what you have is an eating disorder, talk to someone. I have gathered that each case is unique in the ways it appears to play out externally, but inside, it always feels like hell.

We are bombarded by the most current fad diets at all times. Living where I live and doing what I do for a career does not help. I have to try extremely hard to not allow diet culture to consume me. Overhearing conversations about what women are doing to cut carbs and how bananas are too sugary (what the actual fuck though? It is a goddamn banana) is something I put up with. I try my best not to add to the narrative by resisting openly discussing my goals and what I am snacking on these days. It is also crucial that we not comment on each other's bodies anymore, you guys. Once I was restricting rigorously following a holiday season, and a few weeks in I had about five different people in one day "compliment" me on my "weight loss" and my figure. Little did they know, I was starving. This streak of feedback made me feel so intensely aware of my body shape that I spiraled out of control in the opposite direction and engaged in spells of binge eating (likely my body also trying to revert to normal).

We live in our bodies. We do not need other people telling us what they see; it distorts our already-damaged perception of ourselves. Keep it to yourself, girlfriend. If I look hot, tell me I look hot, dammit! Tell me you love my hair; tell me I look happy if I do. Do *not* tell me I look skinny minny.

I can only speak to my experience, so I will chime in one more time with the *hey, you, seek professional help, please!* nudge. For me, my eating disorder feels like a ruthless bully. I joke that my eating disorder has a similar persona to those brash, aggressive aunts who yell all the time in *The Handmaid's Tale*. I am Offred, except way less brave, heroic, badass, and

I definitely cannot pull off granny panties the way Elisabeth Moss can. My eating disorder is Aunt Lydia. She punishes me and isolates me from the people and activities that I love. She acts on the fallacy that she has my best interest at heart. Some days more than others, but nearly every time I walk by a mirror, my eating disorder whispers to me a soft, familiar, *stop eating*. A disease of the mind, I tell you. It is dark, lonely, and painful. By putting these words down, I feel less alone and I hope that by reading them, you do too.

My journey of recovery from my eating disorder has felt like an endless internal war filled with violent self-talk and back-and-forth decisions. When I begin to put on (likely unnoticeable to the outside world) a couple pounds due to allowing myself to eat, I become insecure and am immediately tempted to retreat and restrict. I know how to keep the weight off—just be hungry. That is the easier route. The more difficult path is to challenge the thoughts that enter my mind that tell me my crush will never love me because I have dimples on my thighs or can pinch my tummy. Deciding whether or not recovery is worth it is a choice I have tirelessly pondered. Lately, I am so sick of being hungry. I am exhausted of meticulously editing my life to cater to my eating disorder.

The other day I was driving down Ventura Boulevard after work. It was a beautiful Sunday afternoon, around one o'clock. At that time every week, the city of Los Angeles is buzzing with the brunch crowd. Alone and on my way to my favorite juicer, I drove by the crowds waiting in line outside the poppin' brunch spots. I observed menus in manicured hands, mimosas being poured on clothed tables, numerous smiles, and shared laughter under the spring sunshine. I want that. I want to sit down at brunch on a Sunday with my friends and not want to die over the thought of eating delicious pancakes. I want to go to a brewery and try the yummy local fare. I want to go on a date with a man and not have to prepare all day long for the couple of drinks I may consume come nightfall. I am sick of being hungry. I am sick of allowing my eating disorder to decide my weekend plans. I am going to get better. I am going to recover. I am going to be happy. I am going to fight this thing, you all as my witnesses.

All of my years of therapy have equipped me with an extremely heightened sense of awareness. I can think logically and I am now cognizant of when I am acting on a disordered thought or behavior. There have been periods of my life where I have gone months without tracking my calories, but time and time again, relapses occur, usually triggered by an unflattering photo of myself in a swimsuit (I SAID NO PICTURES, YOU GUYS!). I have isolated myself from numerous life experiences due to crippling fear of consuming the cuisine that comes along with said events.

On the other hand, I am also proud to say I have fully relished in guilt-free meals as an adult (usually while on vacation. I am currently trying to implement these unmatched moments into my everyday life). Recalling the time I ate a crêpe on the cobblestone streets of Paris without an ounce of regret will always be a victory for me. When my mind is in a healthy place and I am able to tune in and listen to what my body needs, I find that various areas of my life improve significantly. It is crazy what a difference actually eating dinner will make in your mood. While fueling my body properly, I have more energy to dance, play with my dog, and extend my kindness to strangers. When I am not spending every waking moment worrying about sugar content, I create more space and emotional capacity to give the gift of love to others and to myself.

What I can say is this: my life would be better if I had never discovered that app. If you have never counted calories, please, *please* do not start. Kale makes us feel energetic, so yes, eat it! But also go get that margarita with your girls. You need your friends, and they need you too. Find foods that make you feel radiant and bring happiness into your life, but also do not ponder on the subject too much. Your body will tell you what it requires. Listen.

Easier said than done. Trust me, I know.

Roasted Kale is a Pathetic Excuse for a Food: Reprise

As some of you may or may not know, I wrote this book in six weeks starting in March of 2019. Chapter three was actually the first section that my mind hurled out through the keys of my laptop. At the time I initially composed this book, my relationship to food and eating was sticky, complicated, and I was not sure if I would ever be able to change my detrimental restricting habits. Part II of "Roasted Kale is a Pathetic Excuse for a Food" is coming at you live from late June of 2019, my current present day. Writing *Show Me Yours And I'll Show You Mine* was a pivotal moment in my eating disorder recovery. I have now been suffering from my eating disorder for over six years. It troubles me deeply that such a significant percentage of my time on this earth has been spent checking my tummy bloat in the mirror and googling how many calories are in a glass of Cabernet Sauvignon. I mean, for fuck's sake, I could have probably cured cancer by now! Well, maybe not, but you get my point.

Three years into my eating disorder, I realized it was an issue that needed addressing, so if you are as amazing at math as I am, you can conclude that the most recent three years of my life have been spent battling it and honestly, feeling like I am losing most of the time. I have deleted and re-downloaded the MyEatingDisorderPal app numerous times, grappled over how many calories I should be consuming, and engaged in a back-and-forth war in my mind over what the hell I should do. How can I have the body I want but also not go fucking insane? What can I accept and love about my body? Should I just fucking find a new profession and be done with all of this? Maybe I will move to Hawaii, become a meditation guru with natural hair, a tan, and only eat coconuts.

Around the time I wrote this book, I decided it was time to pick up my sword and shield and fight this thing again. I could feel myself growing weary of the dieting, exhausted by the hunger, and overcome by the obsession. I did not want to be sick any more. I eased into intuitive eating by increasing my caloric allowance but still only put "healthy," societally acceptable foods into my body. I began to track less and less until finally, I was able to find it in me to delete the MyEatingDisorderPal app again. I was fortunate that the timing of this aligned with some time off work I had and some traveling I was planning to do. The couple weeks I spent back on the East Coast, not tracking a single calorie, birthed some of the most stunning memories I know will last me a lifetime.

This is the thing about wars. When the enemy realizes you are here and you mean business, it fights back even harder. Even though I am going out and having more fun and living my life with freedom, the enemy seethes with anger and tempts me to return to an unwell state. There are parts of me that are still sick and they speak to me daily. Sick me chimes in to remind me how intoxicating it felt to grow too small for my clothes day after day. Healthy me remembers how luxurious it feels not going to bed starving every night, so I keep going. Sick me sees old photographs from when I was hungry and wishes I were sick again so I could still look like that. Healthy me remembers how much happier my life is now, so I keep going. Sick me tries convincing me that I am unworthy of love because I have dimples on my thighs, and I can pinch my stomach now. Healthy me remembers that I am uninterested in a partner who would prefer sick me over healthy me. Sick me mulls over how easy it would be to just start tracking again for a little while just to lose a few pounds. Healthy me ponders and revels in the true-ass fact that roasted kale is a pathetic excuse for a food.

Eating disorders are tricky because "staying strong" and becoming "healthy" sometimes for us recovering dieters, restrictors, anorexics, bulimics, and so on appear the exact *opposite* of what society has conditioned us to believe those concepts are. The responsible thing for me to do is to gracefully welcome this layer of fat that wants so badly to reside on my tummy. Society, beauty standards, and the dance world want to convince me that that is irresponsible. Every day I have to choose to rise above the toxic messages that have been harshly sent my way for so long.

Hear me when I tell you this: it is worth it. Even though select moments feel impossible, I have lived some of the most carefree moments, even entire days of my life in the recent past, all thanks to this war I chose to partake in. Those beautiful days are my motivation to keep pushing forward. Also, not for nothing, but I have a lovely, voluptuous booty now! So keep going. Do not fucking stop. Stay strong.

Chapter Four

Yup, I Just Tweeted John Mayer Lyrics I'm Fucked

Honestly, I am not even sure what the exact current status of my love life is, so yeah, I can't really give you a proper hint as to what is about to unfold in this chapter. All I really know is that my relationships with men take up what is likely far too much real estate in my mind. I will admit that I daydream about my crushes, my exes, and John Mayer's tattoos more than I would like to, but hey, I am only human. I believe relationships are an extension of who we are as individual beings and we can learn a lot of valuable lessons from them. Buckle up as I word vomit some thoughts to you, my friend. Knowing who we are is essential to functioning as adults but also as adults in partnerships. Think about what makes you, you as you read on about some elements that make me, me.

The Alone Thing

This year I relocated to a studio apartment with my dog. It was always my fantasy to live by myself, free from the burden of worrying about those around me. Codependents have a hard time with roommates because the constant stress of inhibiting another and invading their living space (although, hello, it is mine too, silly) can be too much to take. If you are anything like me, there is nothing more soul-sucking than finally returning home from work to find that your roommates have company over. This new place that I completely cannot afford is a dream come true. I can now isolate myself and do weird shit for hours on end and no one will notice!

As we have gone over, my parents love me a lot. What a complaint, right?! It is almost comical how consistently they are there for me. I believe this to be one of the reasons I value personal space so highly. I instantly grow sheepish when someone wanders into the kitchen while I am binge eating almond butter or even cooking something completely respectable. I do not like eyes on me in my natural habitat—I only want you adoring me from afar, through your phone screen on Instagram, or from the audience of a show I am dancing in. Talking to people after shows has always made me very uncomfortable. If this book ever gets published and you meet me at a signing, go easy on me—I appreciate you, but human interaction (especially where I feel like I have to live up to expectations) is incredibly draining for me. I would much prefer an adoring fan letter from you so I can read it over and over again for some much-loved validation while in the safety of my own home, on my couch with no bra on.

There is a small handful of humans I feel as though I do not have to live up to any expectations around, and thank God for them. I do not depart interactions with them feeling drained. Rather, I leave them feeling enriched. Sometimes it is hard for me to get my ass off my daily routine and make time to see them, but I live in an infinite cycle of reminding myself that isolation is detrimental to mental health. Being around those we love is a proven psychological need. Do it up, loners!

Today, I have spent the entire day alone (with the exception of my dog; thank you, Jesus) and around 4 p.m., I began to feel the sting of loneliness, so I pulled out my dating apps. Dating is exhausting for introverts. I do not particularly enjoy meeting new people at all. What currently motivates me is not meeting them but learning more about myself by observing how I react to them. Selfish, I know. Because I am all about honesty, maybe my Tinder bio should read, "Hey there, you are probably disappointing, but I like to learn about myself through human interaction, so shall we give it a go?" It is almost impossible to scrape up the motivation to open your comfortable little world to new people when you are so content on your own.

I will always be a fan of star-fishing my queen-sized bed and being the only person with access to my chocolate-covered almonds that reside in the pantry. It is even harder to go out and look for a mate when you already have a few friends who deeply, intrinsically understand you. When you feel complete and whole on your own, why the hell would you bring someone else into the mix to disrupt your peace? Dopamine and oxytocin, I guess. *Sigh* *Opens Hinge*

The Together Thing

You know how they say too much of a good thing makes it go bad? As noted in chapter one, I live for extremes. When I am alone, I am painfully, completely, hard-core mother-fucking alone. When I am in love, I want you so much I can barely breathe! I do not think I can let any of my chapters go by without mentioning how much I love and seek male approval. It is the main issue I am working on right now at twenty-three. It is so pathetic to me, and that is precisely why I am fighting against it to the death. I have a lot of fucking feelings. I identify far too closely with that girl in the movie *Mean Girls* who wears the red polo and talks about baking cakes of rainbows and sunshine. I love love so goddamn much it hurts. Watch out, dudes; if you DM me once, I will assume you want to get married. I realized I was in over my head with Adrenaline Guy when he said one bare-ass minimum sweet thing that might have indicated that he possibly cared even the slightest bit about me. The next day I was tweeting John Mayer lyrics. Why? I guess infatuation and loneliness could be to blame for dragging me deep into the rhythmic waves of lust. I hang onto even the smallest of affections men shoot my way. How can we fix this? I am currently stumped. As I go through my single days, I am steadily probing for someone to receive even a microscopic dopamine hit from. I try not to be too hard on myself because as a species, we are biologically programmed for companionship. I do wish, though, that I could find a little more tranquility on the days one of my many crushes does not look my way.

I want to tell you guys a little story. So if I may, there was once forty-eight hours of my life when a man made me feel absolutely batshit crazy. To me, it is a tale worth telling because unfortunately, I witness so many intelligent people fall victim to emotional manipulation. Experiencing extreme inconsistency from a romantic partner actually had me convinced there was something wrong with *me*! I learned a lot from this short-lived but emotionally intense experience.

All right, friends, so this guy and I had been communicating digitally for a couple months. We had some mutual acquaintances and soon after he got out of a relationship, he was blowing up my scene. I approached with caution because, not to brag, but emotionally unavailable men seeking distraction and solace are sort of my thing. Men who are heartbroken flock to my Instagram DMs for some reason. It is like there is a huge neon sign on my page that reads "I'll save you!" Either that or they have noticed in some of my photos that I have huge boobs. Anyway, I was not taking it very seriously at all, knowing he was so freshly single. I did not entertain the attention much at first, certain he was saying the same things to every other cute girl he followed on social media.

The attention and validation kept coming, which I totally did not mind. Who can blame a gal, right? Sometimes when I was high or a little tipsy, I would respond and make witty comments that I got a kick out of. This progressed for weeks and once he had been ridin' solo for what seemed to be a substantial amount of time, we began having real conversations. I was even transparent with him about how I definitely noticed how rapidly he went from posting photos with his girlfriend to responding to my hot photos saying things like "well marry me now." Eye roll, right?

Anyway, I grew to enjoy talking to this guy. He would text me almost every day, ask what I was up to, and give me those much-adored compliments. I was lonely as hell and I was attracted to his persistence and what seemed to be the qualities of an alpha male who got what he wanted. Of course, in retrospect I understand that he was simply what we ladies refer to as a "reply guy" (a dude who seeks attention wherever he can get it by replying to any and all of the cute Instagram stories by literally every one of the opposite sex).

But at the time, I found our conversations amusing. They actually contained substance, openness, brutal honesty, and humor. I did some social media stalking and was able to conclude that this guy was in fact attractive and probably someone I would be into. I even heard his voice on some of the videos he sent me and it was deep and sexy. With the context of our mutual friends and me actually knowing his ex was a cool girl, I landed on the decision that he could not be that bad, right? In my book, homie had passed the "guy I met on the internet" screening. After a couple months of these fun flirtations, we decided to meet up on the Fourth of July, a holiday that holds a lot of history and a ton of weight for me. Am I the only one?

The beaches of southern California were humming with the tipsy excitement of sand, beach balls, and White Claws. The sun was lovingly beaming down on us and there was not a parking spot in sight. I love where I live. Anyway, there he was, looking tan and delicious, the man whose eye I had caught and the man who had not run away when he began regularly viewing my crude, ridiculous Snapchat stories. I know I deserve the world, but at the time, I had not been interested in someone like this in a while so the feeling I got when I met him was almost too good to be true. Apparently, it was.

Homie was even more physically attractive to me in person, so Mama was pumped. I was slightly overwhelmed and began to grow a little nervous, checking with my friends throughout the day to make sure I still looked slammin'. It was so difficult for me to get a read on this dude, which caused me to pull my attention away from my own experience and fixate it on his. A big no-no I have been working on. He was not so much the flirty alpha he had painted himself out to be. He hardly took charge or made an effort to spend time with me at the party *he* invited me to. Of course, I took it personally, wondering if I had somehow been disappointingly shorter in person or if I talked too much. I was on a mission to determine if I was somehow not what he expected. Because I was not receiving the attention I had anticipated from him, I craved it even more deeply. As the day went on, I found myself verbally touching base with him to see where his head was at as an attempt to evaluate the situation as if it were one of those thousand-piece puzzles I could never solve as a child.

Believe me when I tell you that homie's signals were MIXED. And no, not like a fun vodka drink. More like a tornado causing mass destruction in this pretty little head of mine. In the moment, I was lost in his tan skin, hanging onto the fleeting instances when he'd place a hand on my hip and ignoring the ones where he made me feel like I was no longer interesting enough to hold his attention. There I was, flooded with confusing emotions, in too deep, and in over my head.

After quite a few drinks, we hooked up. It was fine. We both wanted to and had discussed that it might happen even prior to actually meeting in person. At this point, I thought I had fully drawn him in, but I was wrong. The rest of that hot summer day, quite a beautiful one as a matter of fact, went about the same as it did before we had some steamy alone time. His nonchalance perturbed me. In some instances, I felt out of place and as though I should just leave the party and go home. In others, we were giggling together and even though I knew we were not going to get married, I gathered we were having fun and that's what I was there for, right? Moments of extreme longing and discomfort were overpowered by the rush of dopamine and oxytocin that flooded my brain when he put his arms around me. I stuck around the party because I do not feel this type of excitement about everyone. I wanted to see it through.

I do not have an issue with putting myself out there and being vulnerable, so at the end of the night, I told him I liked him. I enjoy transparency and much prefer to put all my cards on the table and air out my dirty laundry for the world to see (as you can tell by this book). So yeah, under the night sky lit up with fireworks, as we were kissing goodbye, "Fuck! I like you!" slipped passed my lips. He smiled, a great smile by the way, kept his arms around me, chuckled a little bit, and replied, wait for it ..."You're fun." HA! You guys, this was such a humorous response, I honestly give him credit. I hope it makes you laugh too.

He proceeded to instruct me to please to text him when I got home safe, blah blah blah, and I was like okay, yes, will do. Good night, okay, bye, blah blah blah. Now, I was not really surprised by his response. Sure, it stung, but it was truly the reply I had anticipated due to how the day unraveled. It was a confirmation that my instincts were right all along. I did not tell Homeboy I liked him because I wanted to hear that he liked me too. I told him because I was excited, shocked, and happy to feel that way towards someone. It had been a minute.

Although I was not taken off guard that Homeboy was unable to express any type of affection towards me outside of the bedroom, I could not help but be disappointed. I was rip-roaring drunk on the high of being genuinely, fully into someone, not having to fake anything or dismiss a weird mannerism or something I was not fully attracted to. I was abruptly forced to confront the reality that it had to end that night. As my mind assessed the collateral damage, I wondered if I had come on too strong or if my humor was too out there or if I had overstayed my welcome. I feared that he thought I was too intense and crazy for even a simple friends-with-benefits situation.

July 5th was a nightmare. I was hungover and sleep-deprived, coupled with the bad taste left in my mouth from the night before, creating a stomach-churning meatloaf recipe for disaster. I was crashing from the oxytocin high from his kisses and mourning how wonderful my insides felt every time he laughed. Dammit was I in deep. I wondered if I should reach out and apologize. I even typed a note on my phone of what to say. I completely and unquestioningly blamed myself.

I have an addictive personality. We know this. When I get a taste of something that gets me the high I want to feel all the time, I nearly feel like I am going to die when I experience the come down. People sometimes do not understand me when I say this, so I am searching for the best way to explain it. I am aware of the fact that I do not actually depend on men. I am a strong, independent woman. Can I get a hell yeah? But, and there is a but, men get me intoxicated and I am an addict. *I do want to take a moment to acknowledge the fact that I do not use the word addict lightly. Coming from a family with an intense history of addiction and knowing what my parents do for a living, I want to be sensitive to the community of recovering addicts. Those with chemical dependency addictions fight a battle I cannot even begin to fathom.

I refer to myself as an addict because if the man I am fixated on does not reciprocate my love, my insides feel like they begin to shrivel up. I long for and crave his affection and my mind will not allow me to ponder any other subjects. An extremely intrinsic, primitive chemical shift occurs in my brain when my guy decides not to text me on any random given day. Do I know this is illogical? Yes. But do I feel it anyway? Yes. Sometimes my life feels dull without a romantic love interest to fixate on. Do I know this is unhealthy? Yes. Am I working on it? I am trying my fucking best. I have been so down in the dumps and have felt so shitty from boy withdrawal that I have questioned my own mental health and dependence. I have taken quizzes on the twelve-step sites and have come to the conclusion that yeah, I probably should check out an SLAA and/or an Al-Anon meeting at some point. This issue of mine has only come to my attention recently and I am still in the process of deciding exactly how I am going to deal with it.

Back to Homeboy. I was convinced it was my fault that the outcome of my one-day romance with Homeboy was less than ideal. I squirmed around the entire next day feeling lost, shitty, and undesirable. Because I was so depressed, I felt as though there was something wrong with me. That my oxytocin addiction made me unworthy of love, connection, and the common courtesy of communication. Thankfully, I have great friends and I reached out to one that lived nearby who also attended the party with me the day prior. I went over everything out loud, from the months leading up to the party, then the party itself, excavating for what I could have possibly done wrong. I had exposed him to my sense of humor a million times before meeting. I looked cute, am fun to talk to, and overall a great catch (we've been over this!) so I could not figure out where I had made an error.

"You did not do anything wrong. That's why you are so stumped," my friend Cait assured me over and over again even when I swore I disagreed. Thank God for friends, seriously. We get so blinded by our emotions that we lose the ability to assess clearly. When you feel crazy, go plant your sunburned ass at your BFF's kitchen table while she makes spaghetti squash and talks you off the ledge. "You are not crazy." Why did I feel so insane?

"He did a one-eighty on you, girl. You were acting accordingly based on the history the two of you had. He was the one not aligning with previous conversations." Oh. Yeah. My mind had completely ignored the joke he made a week earlier about wanting to be my boyfriend or how he constantly pressed me for information, expressing interest in what I did for a living and who I was. I immediately assumed *I* was acting crazy. Meanwhile, *he* was the one behaving out of character and, possibly unconsciously (I like to give people the benefit of the doubt), using manipulative behavior to string me along all day.

Now, deep breath. This guy seriously does not deserve a feature in my book. I am frustrated with myself for even having needed to bat an eyelash and ponder over this brief encounter. He has not done anything momentous to earn so many pages here, but let me assure you that this section of my book is not about him. It is about you, reader, and me. Sure, he had a tattoo and nice facial scruff, but he was unpredictable and his inconsistency caused me turmoil that we can all learn from. The way he would change the subject when I asked him how he was enjoying single life, and the pure fact that at times he made me feel as though he genuinely liked me and other times he did not, all prove that he had a lot of unaddressed emotional shit he needed to work out on his own. *And* Homeboy obviously had poor judgment because, as we have been over, ya girl is a total catch.

Anyway, back to us. *Never* apologize for being vulnerable, leading with your heart, and bringing your true self to the table. Those who disapprove do not earn a seat at said table. I am an incredibly self-aware person who is constantly in tune with the world around me and for forty-eight hours there, I was convinced I was truly mad. At twenty-three, I am proud to know a lot about myself and the way I operate. But all of that went out the window due to Homeboy's inconsistency.

Listen up now, ya hear? Use logic to pay attention to *who* in situations is acting out of character. Talk things out with your friends and/or therapist from start to finish. Include all details and get their opinions. Trust yourself—if a romantic partner makes you feel crazy, there is probably something wrong with him or her, not you. Remember, you *cannot* save or fix anyone! Trust me, I would love to do a full workup, analysis, and diagnosis to figure out precisely why Homeboy treated me the way he did, but the truth of the matter is that his well-being is simply not my responsibility. Please *do not* lose sight of your value for NO MAN and finally, for Christ's sake, please stay away from Geminis ;).

The Feels

I am an artist. We thrive on feelings. Feelings pay our rent. There is an Amy Winehouse quote I love that I heard in one of the documentaries that was created honoring her life. She says, "When you write a song, you have to remember what you felt. You might have to remember what the weather was like. You might have to remember what his neck smelled like. You have to remember all of it." I was channeling this painful reality recently when choreographing a new project. I had painted a picture in my mind of how awesome it would be to fall in mutual, blissful love with one of my unavailable romantic interests. It was evident that we were not going to be together, but I straight-up pretended for the sake of my project.

This probably sounds familiar to artists but batshit crazy to non-artists. I knew this hopeful thinking was potentially damaging, but the need to create work that came from a genuine place was more important to me. It is hard to cut myself off from my fantasies of love that does not exist because it feeds my art so well. It is also painful and slightly maddening, so hmm, maybe some balance would be good? As much as I love my impossible fantasies, I am so thankful for the cognitive behavioral therapy I have received because it has given me the ability to question my thoughts and pull me back to shore when I have fallen in too deep again. Once the dance is choreographed and set, I am able to come back down from my world of fluffy feelings and land back into my reality which is very, very alone.

The Apart Thing

When I think of relationships, I cannot help but relive their endings. All of my previous relationships have ended, obviously, so looking back sometimes feels grim. Even if the relationship did not tarnish in madness and heartbreak, I still dread that awful conversation when it must be terminated. When I need to get out of a relationship, the first clue I receive is from my gut. My stomach instantly informs me when something is not right. Thankfully, I have always been very in tune with my body, so it is impossible for me to ignore these visceral and intrinsic sensations. People always criticize those who think with their heart and not their head, but I disagree. My body has never lied to me. My stomach alerts me when I am in danger and when I am safe. My head lies to me every damn day. My head tells me I am fat, untalented, and insufferable.

I will say it one more time, because I want you guys to get this—your gut does not lie to you. Your head does. Your head may convince you to stay with the guy because, aw, his family is great and we live together and there is no turning back now! Meanwhile, your stomach drops every time he mentions that vacation you are going to take next year or commitments like getting married or having kids. Listen to your bodies, friends.

Breakups are devastating, I know. They feel like a death. Your gut will never steer you wrong though. Do not stay with someone because you are comfortable or because he is a "good guy." If something feels wrong, do not ignore that. The revelation that you need to get out is the absolute worst; my stomach is churning just thinking about when I have encountered these moments in the past. I recall predictable evenings on couches sitting next to my significant other for the millionth time, being faced with the reality that deep down, I was not happy. It sucks, especially when you do truly love someone. Breakups are a part of the whole deal though, guys; you have to do it. Who knows; maybe you will get a whole book's worth of content out of it like I did!

In addition to the pain of letting go of someone who was once so close to you, it becomes difficult to muster up the motivation to love again when this deep sadness is what you remember about love. All we can do is keep moving forward, I guess, and chase the good feels. My rule of thumb is this—if it feels good today, we keep it! The day it feels bad (I am not talking a disagreement or a fight, of course. Those are normal) deep down in your gut, we do not keep it any more. Chasing my feelings has steered me right thus far, so tap into those feels, my good people.

The other day I took a solo beach trip. Bummed that all of my friends were unavailable to come along, I was beginning to grow sorry for my single self. What a perfect day it would have been to have a boyfriend! The self-pity party lasted a little while until I settled in on my blanket, pulled out my trail mix, and began watching the lull of the waves. I then attempted to put things into perspective. I was lonely in that moment but reminded myself of all of those tired expressions that are permanently seared into my brain. *The grass is never greener; there is no time like the present, baby; carpe diem!*

I may have been in deep with my feels, but guess who was there to rescue me from drowning? Me! Being there at the beach alone was significantly more peaceful than getting screamed at by a significant other for parking too far away or forgetting to pack their protein bar. I actually happened to be chillin' at the beach with my favorite person on earth, me. I am the one who understands me better than anyone else can. I do not have to soften my sense of humor around me. I get me like no one else does. No witty thought of mine is too crude. No emotion is too scary, extreme, or intense to where I have to minimize it in order to protect the feelings of someone else.

I do not have to put up a façade around myself; I love and accept every weird bit and part of me. I do not have to worry about whether or not who I am with is having a pleasant day or consider when they want to leave or wonder if they are hungry; it is just me. I am hopeful that someday I will be able to experience this type of raw intimacy and pure, unconditional acceptance with someone else, but for now, I have me. And that is all I need.

Chapter Five

Ever Have a 2½-Year-Long Herpes Scare?

Ah yes, I wish it were not true, but you did read that correctly. The Lord gives his toughest battles to his strongest soldiers, right? Let me set this very romantic and glamorous scene for you (she said sarcastically). It was a beautiful, crisp, sunny winter day in Buffalo. I had just turned twenty-one. I was finally getting good at having partnered orgasms and was soon to be graduating college. Life was good. I remember sitting at my kitchen table in my shared apartment when I got the phone call. It was a female voice, youthful and sweet. When she asked if she could speak with Rachel Hospers and informed me that she was calling from my OBGYN's office, my stomach dropped. I had been going for routine checkups and screenings for many years and they had never once called me after a visit in the past. "No news is good news!" they'd always say.

I can remember what the nurse's voice sounded like, but I do not remember much else from the conversation we exchanged. I can hear her asking me if I had any questions. I responded, "Not right now, no. I will call if I think of any." My vision went a little fuzzy as I zoned out into the tan-speckled countertop of my kitchen table. HSV-1. Herpes Simplex Virus 1. Oral herpes. As always, that year at my appointment they had taken a cotton swab culture of my uterine tissue (yum). What I assumed happened was that they found traces of the HSV-1 virus in my lovely downstairs area during my pap smear, meaning I was diagnosed with HSV-1, but in the genital region.

In case you are not aware, herpes is common as hell and there are two different strains of the virus. Herpes Simplex Virus 1 (or HSV-1) is known as the oral strain. Now, I was never great at science, but this still does not make much sense to me because you can contract HSV-1 in your oral region and/or your genital region, but the *majority* of orally located herpes (a.k.a. cold sores) are caused by HSV-1. Herpes Simplex Virus 2 (or HSV-2) is known as genital herpes, which you can also contract in your oral region and/or your genital region, but the *majority* of genitally located herpes cases are caused by HSV-2.

The World Health Organization (WHO) classifies HSV-2 as a sexually transmitted infection because it more commonly causes genital herpes. I did some research and according to the World Health Organization, in 2017, an estimated 3.7 billion people under age fifty (sixty-seven percent) had HSV-1 infection globally. So yeah, extremely common. Many are born with it, and many get it from common oral-to-oral contact. When I spoke with my OBGYN recently, she rounded up to seventy-five or eighty percent because so many cases do not show symptoms. Noted in the same article I found on the WHO's site, four hundred and seventeen million people aged fifteen to forty-nine (eleven percent) worldwide were estimated to have the HSV-2 infection in 2017.

Every year when I visited my gynecologist, she routinely offered to take a blood sample for some more in-depth STI screening. At twenty-one, I thought the blood test was just for HIV, the virus that causes AIDS. She always talked so freaking fast. She'd be like, "Would you like to do the blood test this year to screen forHIVandsiugaqwiuyoi?" I opted for the additional blood work that year for the first time in my life, mostly because I had had a couple more sexual partners since my last test. I figured, "I'll take the lot! Give me the works! Let's do it all, why not?"

When I received that phone call a few days later, something about the way she worded the results had my naive little mind convinced that the virus was without a doubt identified from the pap-smear test, not the blood, since I thought the blood test was only to test for HIV. A lot of the time, HSV-1 and HSV-2 are commonly diagnosed when a patient is facing discomfort due to a breakout. Doctors take a skin sample from the blisters of an active breakout and can diagnose it that way. Because there is no cure for either virus, traces of it live on in the blood even when there is not an active breakout. Due to my lack of knowledge on the subject and the way that the brief conversation with the nurse went, I gathered that my HSV-1 was detected in the cotton-swab culture they took that year and therefore was genital herpes even though I had never had a breakout or any symptoms at all. I don't know, guys. I am not a doctor, and I most certainly was not a doctor at twenty-one, so I did the best I could with the information that I had.

So, I informed my boyfriend at the time that I had genital HSV-1. We were attending separate universities so I brought it up to him in person when he was next up for a visit. I was nervous, timid, and felt slightly ashamed. It was a subject that was looming over my mind. When he first got to town that weekend, we spent time with friends. So finally, when we got to be alone, I was able to have a proper conversation with him about it. He handled the information I presented like a champ.

He was warm, loving, and accepted the fact that it could have even quite possibly been from him since he had not ever been tested for HSV. Later he informed me that I was so serious and formal when initiating the conversation, he was worried it was something more serious. I had done a ton of research and learned about the facts and statistics I presented in the previous paragraph. It's not common, but you can contract HSV-1 on your genitals if someone who has an active cold sore performs oral sex on you. That's how I assumed I got it, if not from my boyfriend at the time, from one of my other most recent partners. My boyfriend and I had been sexually active for a while and neither of us was showing symptoms, so we just carried on as we had been for the rest of our relationship; business as usual.

I am not going to lie, at twenty-one, the thought of an STI was heartbreaking. At that age, I felt as though I was just getting started having fun, enjoyable sex and then bearing this news was quite devastating. I had only had four sexual partners at the time, but I still felt like I had somehow deserved this by being reckless and promiscuous. All the untrue, rude-as-fuck thoughts that I imagine anyone who has an STI has entered my mind. *You don't deserve love because you have herpes. You are a bad person because you have herpes. You did this to yourself.*

In case you are not aware, herpes is one of the only sexually transmitted infections that does not have a cure. Why couldn't my first STI be something like chlamydia? Just some cute antibiotics and then we're good to go! I looked around at my peers and envied the way they talked about their seemingly spontaneous sexual encounters. Out the door went my dream of someday attending a weird sex club in a mask or whatever. I was young, insecure, and took everything personally, so this diagnosis certainly did not boost my self-esteem. As time passed and I did more research, I found out how common genital HSV actually is and how many people live with it.

As I got a little bit older, being comfortable with who I was became easier, so in turn, my appreciation and value for myself grew as well. I learned more and more about how to talk about sex and how to be comfortable voicing my desires and feeling good in my own body. I never had a breakout or any symptoms at all and I was in a monogamous relationship, so it really was not a bother at all; it was the social stigma that got to my head.

Things got interesting a couple years later when that boyfriend and I broke up and I was single for the first time since that awful fucking phone call. I now had to learn how to tell new sexual partners that I had genital HSV-1. The thought of voicing this to a new, unfamiliar lover I was trying to win over put a pit in my stomach. I agonized over the day I would have to say the words. I was not excited to find new sexual partners; I was dreading them. So I did what I could. I educated myself on the risks.

Shout-out to Google. You are most likely to transmit any form of HSV during and immediately after a breakout, so it is best to avoid sex during those times. *Okay,* I thought, *I have never had a breakout, so we are good there*! You are most likely to transmit HSV the first year after you contract it. I was also good there; it had been two years. So for me, the chances of a partner getting it from having sex with me were pretty slim. There is also a medication you can take that clears breakouts and suppresses the virus, lowering a partner's risk even further. I had my doctor prescribe me a bottle so I could take these leading up to times I suspected I might be sexually active.

So yeah, when I was sleeping with a new partner, I would always try and squeeze in all of that painfully unsexy information before we had sex. I usually said something like this: "Hey, so, this is what it is, and these are your risks … I always like to inform my partners because apparently someone didn't tell me and that sucks!" Did it kill the vibe? I'll be honest, yes. But only for a moment. I'll let you in on a little secret. One hundred percent of the times I had this conversation with men, they always still came a few minutes later. So it can't be that bad, right? Ha ha.

You can totally still have a great sex life, I promise. I never regretted telling anyone about my status. Mature guys who were educated on the topic reacted impeccably. If anyone were to ever think negatively about me after learning I had an STI, that is a reflection on their character, not mine. What I did by speaking up is respectable as fuck. I pride myself on the way I handled my sexual encounters during that time of my life.

Still fairly new into the adult single life post-diagnosis, I was not too worried about my HSV-1 until I had my first iffy reaction from a sexual partner. I am not going to go too far into detail because it was not blatant shaming or anything of that nature, more of just a tiny gut feeling that I was being judged by this new partner. Follow-up conversations with this guy did not sit well with me. Because of this, I felt bummed about the HSV-1 for the first time since being single. That week I brought it up to my therapist. I told her the story of how I was diagnosed, just like I told you guys. She immediately questioned the facts I was so sure about.

"Sorry, I am not an OB-GYN, so I am not positive, but I am pretty sure for it to be genital HSV-1, they would have had to take the culture from a sore, and it seems interesting you were diagnosed without ever having a breakout for them to evaluate," she pressed.

"Hmm, the conversation was almost three years ago now, so I can't recall exactly what they said. I know I had a blood test that year, but for some reason I thought they found traces of the virus in my vaginal culture," I responded.

"Yeah, 'cause, from what I understand, if they just found it in the blood that means you just have the virus like seventy-five percent of the population does. It's not necessarily in your genitals," she said.

Suddenly, in her office, what I thought I knew for so long became muddy. My therapist helped me see that I actually didn't know shit, as she so often does.

"It might not hurt to get tested again, or to call your doctor," my therapist encouraged. "Just so you can ask a couple questions and get complete clarity, so we know exactly what we are dealing with."

I left therapy feeling so dumb. I realized that I was basing so much on a phone call I could hardly remember. Sure, I had done my research on the internet, but I had not talked to my doctor about it. So I thought about it for a few days. Maybe it was time to find a vag doc in LA. Maybe I should go to a clinic and get tested again. (I did read about reports of false positives online too.)

A few days later, I was lying on my couch, feeling pretty shitty. My back was injured at the time, I was battling some nasty acne, and this STI was now in my stream of consciousness more than it had been since the initial phone call from the nurse so long ago. I looked at my phone to check the time. 1:34 p.m. So back on the East Coast, it was 4:34 p.m. My OB-GYN's office would still be open. My therapist's advice danced in my head. I might as well just call them and ask to speak with a nurse to go over my records. A woman answered the phone. She sounded middle-aged and happy. I was instantly comforted by that subtle Upstate New York twang; we like to draw out our A's.

"Hi, I was wondering if you could pull up some lab results from 2016?" I asked.

"Absolutely, just give me a second," she responded.

Once they were ready, I asked, "So that HSV-1 diagnosis from that year, was that gathered from the blood test or from the vaginal culture?"

"They found that in the blood test, honey," she confidently answered.

I began to laugh. *What the actual hell?* What I actually said aloud was more follow-up questions. "Oh really? For some reason I thought it was the other way around. So since it's from the blood, that just means I have HSV-1 lingering around in my body? It is not considered a genital virus?"

"No, sweetie." We giggled together and she continued, "You are fine. It is what seventy-five percent of adults have. Like if you have ever gotten a cold sore in your mouth, it will show up in the blood, that's all."

I swear to you guys, my jaw hit the floor and I bore an uncontrollable ridiculous, toothy grin. I thanked her graciously and hung up the phone. I was sweating alone in my apartment and my heart was racing. God-fucking dammit was I happy I made that phone call! That blood test in 2016 was the first one I had ever had in my life so it was the first I had ever heard of HSV-1. I could have been born with the damn thing in my blood. I could have gotten it from kissing my first boyfriend at age thirteen. These options were far more likely than me having a rare instance of contracting it sexually from one of the four partners I had had at twenty-one, three of which were monogamous relationships. I have never had a breakout of any kind on my genitals and I can't even remember ever having a cold sore in my mouth. What I have is not even considered a sexually transmitted infection because most people get it without having sex of any kind. You probably have it too, my friend! No biggie.

Anyway, back to how dumb I felt. I could not believe I was so, so wrong for so long. I could not believe I had wasted so much unnecessary grief and stress on this topic. In my defense, the nurse who called me in 2016 should have been clearer, especially knowing she was speaking with a patient so young. The physician assistant who prescribed me Valacyclovir (the virus suppressant I mentioned earlier) when I first hopped out onto the dating scene should have pulled up my chart and read the details before writing me the medication. But, admittedly, a lot of this was on me. I failed to ask enough questions. At twenty-one, I clearly was not comfortable speaking with my doctor about these matters. I should have dug for more answers regarding my health, but I did not know how so I resorted to WebMD.

When I told my therapist the great news that I did not have genital herpes, we both could not help but laugh at the situation, thank God. You can too. Go ahead, laugh. I still am. Yep, for over two years, I thought I had genital herpes, *told* people I had genital herpes, all the while not having genital herpes. That's pretty damn funny. It is a silly story, and it has a happy ending—ya girl getting to have spontaneous sex again! So luckily, if nothing else, I learned a lot from this whole damn mess. I learned about both types of HSV through my research. I am now able to be more careful and safer in my sexual experiences. I know what symptoms to look out for and what preventative measures to take. Moving forward, I know more about myself and how to communicate in both the bedroom and in the doctor's office! I also know that if I were to ever contract anything in the future, it would not be the end of the world and I would be okay.

As embarrassing as this story is, I do not have regrets and am proud to tell it because of how I was able to look out for the people I was sleeping with. I cared about them and demonstrated the utmost respect for them with the information I had and so innocently believed was true. So, if you were lucky enough to be a sexual partner of mine during that time and we had that rehearsed conversation, what can I say? Whoops, sorry, baby. If you got herpes, it's probably not from me. Sure, I am upset with twenty-one-year-old me for not figuring her life out, but I am hella proud of twenty-three-year-old me for taking the initiative and making that simple call just to get some clarity. Yeah, I feel stupid for not questioning my mysterious, symptomless "STI" sooner, but it is pretty badass I was able to when I did.

I also wanted to totally humiliate myself with this story because I think it is about goddamn time that we destigmatize herpes. If you remember those stats I listed for you earlier, you know that so many adults are living with HSV-1 or HSV-2 and it's fucking fine, guys. As long you are informing partners of the risks and being good fucking people, there is no harm done. You can have a great sex life and you deserve it! Take pride in the fact that you are on top of your health. Definitely get the facts from your doctors first. Don't be like twenty-one-year-old me or you could end up being sweet, but overly cautious if you base your fate off an assumption. You have nothing to be ashamed of. Learning how to speak up in bed is a useful tool for all of us. If you can't be open and honest with the person you are exchanging love juices with, who *can* you be open and honest with?!

And finally, be safe and get tested, you guys! I am sick of asking men when is the last time they have been screened and getting "uuuhhhhh" as a response. No matter who you are, get tested! It is the considerate thing to do for yourself and your partners. Safe sex is sexy sex! Yay! Have fun out there, kids.

Chapter Six

Is Being Used Still Being Used If You Like It?

Chains and whips do excite me, but masochism turns out to be far more complicated and messier than a 2010's era Rihanna song might suggest. I have done a lot of soul searching, curious as to why I am so attracted to torment given my overall healthy upbringing and loving relationship with my parents. I have concluded that I owe a lot of it to my lovely adrenaline addiction, you old reliable fella, you! Another big part of the reason I love self-torture so much is because I find comfort in punishing myself, as I have also previously touched on. Maybe I was also Jesus in another life, rescuing humanity from their sins by being whipped. That was a joke, obviously, and probably a bad one. Do not come for me. I kid around about this because at times it truly does not seem to add up. Maybe I crave the attention I receive from being in pain—my parents were always overly attentive and responsive if I cried or confided in them about what was bothering me.

Late winter is a rainy time here in Los Angeles. One February morning, I awoke with an aching back, a strained ligament in my ankle I had rolled a few days prior (a reoccurring injury for me), a migraine, and loneliness in my heart. Willingly, I had flown across the country with my belongings, away from everyone that made me happy, in the pursuit of a nearly impossible dream. I shuffled around my home in the morning light, anticipating the dance rehearsal I had to attend in a few hours, dreading the thought of physical activity. It got me pondering the harsh reality that I had indeed hand-selected a life that involves constant physical discomfort. I see a chiropractor weekly just to ensure I can move, and I have a physical therapist on speed dial knowing that at any moment, I could require his services. I cannot complain (although complaining is in my top-ten list of favorite things to do) because I live the life I always dreamed I would.

That morning, more areas of my life where I had chosen the painful path began to reveal themselves to me. I am sexually attracted to men who pretty much act like they hate me. If I get the vibe that you are the type of guy who will love me no matter what, I exit that first date immediately. If you fail to respond to my text messages, Mama will keep coming back for more by stalking your Instagram to figure out where you have been, you sexy little mystery, you! The chase is thrilling and we all want what we cannot have from time to time. But for me, it sort of feels like a twisted game. I love a good challenge. Similar to selecting an almost unattainable career, I look for that same quality in a mate.

For a lot of us, and certainly for me, fear has been transformed into a type of pleasure, resulting in many different types of masochism. In the book *The Body Keeps the Score*, Bessel Van Der Kolk discusses the effects of trauma at length. One point that stood out to me was his analysis of repeated, damaging patterns his patients would partake in. He wondered why he saw patients returning to the very source of their pain over and over again. Pain, both physical and mental, causes our bodies to switch into survival mode and perform all sorts of nifty tricks to combat said disturbance. In the moment of suffering a traumatic wound or injury, our brains produce endorphins—a natural morphine to assist us in coping. I am not a neuroscientist, but I am a human with a memory, and dang that shit feels good! This natural high is so great for us feelings-addicts that in order to get another hit, we might chase the origin of the affliction. This may explain why I, and so many of us, pursue partners who do not treat us well. We could potentially be recreating a relationship with a parent, or in my case, a first love who strayed.

While listening to Van Der Kolk's audiobook, I realized that one of the reasons I am attracted to naughty men is due to an underlying desire to duplicate the trauma of being cheated on in order to feel that pain high again. Ah yes, do we remember my first love from chapter one who broke my heart when I was fifteen? Even over the past few years when I was dating faithful men, I would subconsciously engage in behaviors in order to reward myself with this pain high. My body would react as if it was experiencing that first trauma every time my significant other would go out to a party with his guys, or when I would snoop through his belongings. I used to engage in some hard-core stalking to try and gather as much information as I could, as if that would give me any control over the situation. Although I am a control freak and gain intense pleasure out of feeling in control over whether or not my partner will cheat, I am now realizing those behaviors were about more than just control—they were pain-seeking. I was searching deep in my guy's Instagram for something, anything that would give me that juicy hit of adrenaline and the feeling of betrayal I so adore.

So yeah, I have learned to surrender control. So not to worry, fellas; I do not go through phones anymore or blow you up while you are out laughing with your guys about Brad puking up too much beer, nor will I angrily interrogate you about what type of porn you are watching. I am a *dream*, I swear! No one is perfect, though. Nowadays you will still catch me drooling over men who are over six foot, do not call me back, and like every other girl's Instagram selfie except mine. Mmm, something about facial hair, the impressive speed with which you leave my studio apartment after having your way with me, and the occasional tattoo will always make this heart sing!

Bad boys are fun. That is the truth, even if you are not using them to relive a damaging life event. As I previously mentioned though, we must take care of ourselves here, people. Spiraling down a path of self-destruction is so not sexy! Let's be careful and self-aware through the process, shall we? Again, I am not a mental health professional, so please do not engage in any activities that are detrimental to your prosperity—I always recommend seeing a therapist of your own! I swear, Adrenaline Guy should receive commission checks from mine due to the frequency with which I scheduled appointments with her to cope with our relationship.

When I fall for a guy who does not give me the time of day, I am able to keep a level head due to all the confidence I have earned over the years (more on this in chapter seven). But that does not mean I do not go a little fucking crazy. I am so antsy for my guy's attention that my days sometimes seem to revolve around it. To combat this, I try and keep busy and fill my days with things I need to do for myself. I tend to sulk in my pain for a little while, enjoying the wave of heartbreak before moving on. In some ways this is a healthy thing because suppressing feelings is no good either. Check yourself before you wreck yourself though, ladies; you don't want to turn into a stereotypical Taylor Swift album.

I Got a Little Crush

Boy do I love crushing on dudes. I actually love it even more than the reality of being with them. This is because I have a grand old time painting a creative picture of what I think they are like in my head and I envision us living happily ever after together. When I get a crush, I crush *hard*. It is amazing, but it also kinda sucks ass. I also am not one hundred percent sure how this particular pattern emerged. I remember having so much fun in high school and college, giggling about new love interests with my friends, dopamine pulsing through my body at the very thought of the guy. Life is exciting with a crush. I dirty dance to blasted music in my car while thinking about his cute-ass face. The possibility of running into him or even seeing his name pop up in my Instagram story viewers list is enough to put a pep in this girl's step.

I wonder if I am the only one who has a hard time enjoying crushes simply for what they are, though. I ride the high for a few days but then begin to grow sorrowful if they do not grant me the attention I so profoundly crave from them. Why do I always feel the need for it to go somewhere? Why can I not just enjoy the little flutter in my tummy when I see them in passing? My all-or-nothing personality could be at fault. This is absolutely an area where I need to work on my balance. My masochism could also be partly to blame. Adrenaline Guy caused a roller coaster of emotions for me for over a year. One day I would be as giddy as a child in a candy store because he texted me something naughty that made me blush. Days later, I would become frustrated and upset, crashing from the high of having such an extreme crush. I was addicted to the high of being with him while simultaneously being addicted to the low of his neglect.

Another cutie pie caught my eye recently and I found myself quickly spinning out of control, headed towards the emotional patterns I learned with Adrenaline Guy. I had only known him for a couple days and when I heard he might be single, yup, I was car dancing my heart out and giggling with my friends sooner than he could say "so, where are you from?"

Literally the next day, I was on his Instagram page (of course), bumming myself out, digging and convincing myself that he was in fact unavailable. This guy and I living happily ever after was very unlikely to begin with. He was a distant crush of mine and literally everyone else and was somewhat unattainable, so it was probably doomed to fail from the beginning. After we did become friends, I grew frustrated with myself because I was not able to just keep it at the sweet flirtation it was. Instead, I had to emotionally invest right away and psychotically live for any brief form of contact. It was an odd thing I did, and it put me through a vortex of feelings. I love the high and I love the low, what can I say? I am concerned about what will happen to my brand when I mature enough to start crushing on guys who actually are available and don't get back together with their ex-girlfriends or move out of town after flirting with me for a couple weeks.

On a recent girls' weekend with one of my best friends, Samantha, she pointed out that ever since the situation with Adrenaline Guy, I had become noticeably and violently obsessed with any guy that would show up on my radar. I had suspected this, as my recent few fixations seemed to be all I ever talked about or thought about. I could hear myself annoying my friends by chattering endlessly about these guys, but for some reason, I could not quit. Part of this was because these men were so powerful and unattainable, right up my alley. A man's unattainability and unpredictability just causes me to obsess even more. I realized it was becoming a crippling issue when Sam highlighted it and also when I was experiencing depressive episodes and crying on my therapist's couch over men with whom I had never even had a real relationship.

Ever since listening to the audiobook *Women Who Love Too Much* by Robin Norwood, I have diagnosed my fixation with men as an addiction. This has seemed to assist me in tackling the issue by giving it a label and some structure for treatment. I knew that scrolling through my viewer list of my social media stories was an addictive habit and I could feel the chemicals flowing through me while hunting for that name I so craved to see. But what would happen if his name was there? I would feel great for a moment, but in the long-term, it meant nothing. Once that tiny hit wore off, I would be hunting for my next rush immediately. This is addict behavior that was toxic to my well-being as it only fed my obsessions.

Now, any time a thought or fantasy of one of my impossible men comes to mind, I notice it and try not to judge it. Being upset with myself for being boy crazy does not help anything. I simply notice the thought pattern, the feeling that comes along with it, and I tell myself *oh hi, that is just the addiction talking.* Now, I am not sure if you can actually, scientifically be addicted to love or to men, but this concept has helped me wrap my brain around what is going on and in turn assisted me on my way to recover from my condition of "loving too much" as Robin Norwood explains it.

Why do I do this to myself? echoes through my mind over and over again as I wince, recalling which self-inflicted emotional wound I am nursing this week. So why am I only attracted to men that I have an instinct will hurt me? I have outlined a few key points for you babies already, but I think I can also blame the sexiness of novelty for this one. I grew up in a loving, nurturing home where my mother gave me attention, probably too much. To this day, I still grow irritated if she or anyone pays me too much mind. Nothing will get me to shut the door on your face more quickly than you asking too many questions. Get off my case!

I am a mostly patient person, but my pet peeve is when people put their noses too far in my business. Having eyes on me makes me feel uncomfortable because I begin to second-guess my actions. This is why I immediately stop taking a goofy video of myself inside Target when a stranger walks by or my blood fills with insecurity when a roommate walks in on me eating cake frosting out of the jar with my finger again.

Novelty is sexy. We are attracted to what is unfamiliar. Excessive attention was familiar to me in the essential years of my development. I have a hard time spending too much time around my parents as an adult because of the hovering. Now, when a guy shows me even the slightest thought and then quickly pulls away, my mind says, *oooooh what is this?* Unfamiliarity pulls me in and the desire to receive the rest of the scrutiny I am excited by keeps me around. This is a recipe for a fun, adrenaline-filled, damaging emotional race. Fun stuff.

In recent conversations with my therapist, I begged her to please tell me why the fuck I love impossible men so much. We both laughed at this, but she then pointed out my history. My past is chock-full of wanting impossible things and then eventually, getting them. I have always been headstrong and stubborn and as a child I probably got my way too often. Mama gets what Mama wants. I was not cognizant of this until that very conversation with my therapist. Adrenaline Guy was an enigma to me at first. Somehow, I am still not sure how or why, but Mama got what she wanted: him. Even if it was only for a brief period of time.

For many reasons, my ex was not a suitable match for me either. When I met him, we both knew I was moving across the country shortly. This was only one of the many reasons being with him was kind of a crazy idea. I chose an impractical career as an artist—Mama gets what Mama wants. I am not sure if this is just great luck, my amazing personality, God, determination, or a superpower of manifestation I may have, but it has certainly inflicted a fair amount of positive reinforcement. I spot what seems to be an inaccessible guy? Mama wants. Mama gets.

These "impossible" guys are typically unavailable, successful, powerful, and *drool,* tall. These are the qualities of you guessed it, an alpha male. I am often soft-spoken and adorably sweet, but I absolutely do have a strong personality and I am rigid and solid in what I desire. Because I have a trace of alpha female in me, my alpha male needs to be extra alpha so I feel comfortable enough to fully submit the way I like to in relationships. Ultra-alpha males are what I require. Unfortunately (or fortunately, for the masochist in me), ultra-alpha males are usually obsessed with their work, chased around by hundreds of other beautiful women, and emotionally unavailable. Lovely.

Vulnerability

Whether it be oversharing on the internet, saying "I love you" first, or simply going out a tough audition, I flourish in conditions of vulnerability. People sometimes refer to me as bold and part of that is caused by my innate desire to be authentic, seen, and honest at all times. But lately I have come to the conclusion that it is also because I secretly enjoy the sting that rejection administers. There are so many wonderful upsides to being comfortable with vulnerability; risk-taking reaps a bounty. I also believe that putting yourself out there in life allows you to fully feel everything. It is impossible to earn the highs of success if you do not go out on a whim and fail first. It is the same way with love. Vulnerability sometimes causes us to get hurt, though. Mama likey. I love being vulnerable because of the wonderful results that appear in my life, but I also love being vulnerable because I love being burned. Again, I am still trying to figure out why exactly I feel a sick twinge of satisfaction when I look back on the night I spent crying because I told a partner I had fallen in love with him and he replied that he was unable to reciprocate the sentiment.

Rat-race Society and Worship of Productivity

I gather I am not the only one who finds it oddly satisfying when their physical therapist digs with all their might into that strained muscle. It hurts so good that I am forced to stifle laughter. I like pain because it somehow feels productive, like I will be better as a result. My ligament will heal because of the extreme pressure; my butt will be perkier if I suffer through this workout; I will be a better person and be cool enough to write a book because of this heartbreak.

Our society promotes the idea that only after a certain amount of strain and grief will you receive a reward. Suffer through school so you can get a job. Suffer through work so you can make money. On the GRIND, they say. Hustling, baby. Working for the weekend, they post. *I did it for the pizza* reads the workout tank of an unoriginal soccer mom at your gym. We are conditioned to associate pain with pleasure as a society and that is my theory as to why BDSM porn is so popular. Maybe if we all become a little more present in the moment and envision the things we are grateful for whilst on aforementioned grind, we might be able to sober ourselves from the addictive behaviors and people who bruise us.

And yup, you guessed it, I like being choked during sex.

Since I have been reflecting on all of the areas of my life where I am attracted to pain, I have to mention sex. I am young, and I will admit I am still figuring out all of my sexual jams. I have been sexually active for many years but truthfully, I have only been having good sex that I receive enjoyment from for a few years. Discovering what you like in the bedroom is one thing, but training yourself to voice it to your partner is a whole other rodeo. For me, what helps currently is not racing to the grand finale right away. Sometimes I am eager to hit a home run with a new guy, but from a handful of unsatisfying one-night stands that left me feeling gross, I realized that for me right now, it is best to take it slow. Once I feel comfortable with a man, I can properly voice my desires, ask him about his, and as a result, more fun is had by all!

While my take-it-slow tip does not really align with masochism, some of my kinks do. I was sleeping with an older man recently and could tell he had a lot of experience. While figuring each other out in the sack, we discovered that we both loved when he was degrading and demanding of me. This bossy power play aligned with our narrative outside of the bedroom and it was an exhilarating learning experience for me to tap into this role with this man. He was totally committed to leading, and unapologetic in his commands once I told him I liked it. That shit was HOT!

I have a moment tucked away in my spank bank where he was standing over my bed and he motioned and nodded for me to move back and lie exactly where he wanted me. It was an animalistic beacon, sort of like a cue you give to a dog. Now, I am not sure I would ever put on a collar for a man, but the way this behavior naturally flowed out of us when we were together was fucking beautiful. Now, yes, hi, I have probably gone too far and overshared a little too much again. This section will be blacked out in all of my family member's copies of the book because yikes, boundaries!

The reason I bring up that I like being degraded in the bedroom is because it can sometimes be a masochistic quality to want to be so dramatically dominated by your partner. I also think it is a nod to my control-freak personality and my attraction to alphas. In my everyday life, I feel the desire to take charge, lead, and control the shit out of everything. So if I feel safe in the bedroom with a partner, I love surrendering jurisdiction to them. Damn, sis is hot and bothered now! Maybe I should have chosen to write this section in the privacy of my own home rather than in the auto shop while my car is being worked on. Oops.

Chapter Seven

Am I Really Shaving My Legs For This Sunday Audition Right Now?

Are you guys ready for things to get a little cheesy? Alas, we have arrived at the self-love chapter. Here to report on all the sexy tips to utilize in order to love yourself. Surprise, bitch, I bet you thought you'd seen the last of me! Are you disappointed? Maybe I should have brought in a guest speaker for this section because in case you have not figured it out yet, I am no professional. This chapter is not quite the to-do list of suggestions you may have anticipated such as purchasing expensive bath bombs, cutting out all the toxics in your life, and shouting "break up with your girlfriend, i'm bored" by Ariana Grande at the top of your lungs in the back of an Uber with your besties while buzzed on cheap vodka.

Venturing forward in this book together, we will now take a stroll down memory lane, calculating a road map that traces back what has worked for me in building self-love over the past few years. Somewhere along the line, I must have done something right because I went from merely scraping by on validation from lovers and respected professors to laughing at my own jokes, winking at myself in the mirror when nobody is around (and sometimes when they are), and posting excerpts from my book all over the internet because I find it that damn brilliant!

Now, I know it may not seem relevant, but I was never the absolute best at anything growing up. Being raised by parents who are a little too humble bred me to look around myself and only see the ways people seemed so much more elite than I was. I still to this day have an unfailing instinct to assume that if there is someone else in the room with me, they are automatically smarter, funnier, more beautiful, and more talented than I am. I had low self-esteem for as long as I can remember until recent years when I decided I was fed up with the bullshit. Finally, I looked inward and discovered how truly amazing I am.

I know what you are thinking; that's easy for her to say. She's got DDs, long strawberry-blonde hair, and enviable cheekbones. While I am thankful for these physical attributes, trust me when I tell you, society's opinion of you does not mean shit. We all have insecurities. There will always be a flaw to locate. I am grateful that I had an awful haircut and a humorous overbite as a child because it kept my head small metaphorically. Unfortunately, not physically, though. I literally have a large head.

I began to receive attention for being conventionally attractive around the age of fifteen when my braces came off, but lucky for everyone around me, I was still that insecure child with a mullet on the inside until I was approximately twenty-one years old. It is fair to assume I did not truly grasp my own beauty until a few months ago. Even when I was receiving hundreds of Instagram likes and numerous compliments on my Jessica Rabbit Halloween costume, I was struggling with acne that was plaguing my arms and back. My skin issues robbed me of so much precious time of loving myself in my early twenties (more on acne in chapter ten). Despite the physical insecurities I have, caused by body dysmorphia and skin issues, I still believe I am a damn catch. How, you ask? I don't think there is exactly one answer. Let's get down to the bottom of this together.

In order for me to truly have confidence in myself, I had to look inward at what was so awesome about myself beyond my looks. This was a long and grueling but necessary process. Security is fragile when we rely on one single entity, especially one as delicate as physical appearance. Once I came of age, I knew that beauty was fleeting and that inevitably someday, my gorgeous DDs would sag, and wrinkles would draw themselves across my face.

Sometimes, when I had been particularly quiet for a while, if he suspected something was bothering me, if I was deep in thought, or even if we were just enjoying ourselves at a concert, my ex, Tyler, (who we all know and love by now), would look at me and ask, "How YOU livin'?" He has vulnerability issues, so this was his lighthearted way of getting a glimpse inside my mind. God, I hope he approves of this book so I can keep all of these juicy details in here without getting sued or having to address him by a degrading code name (sorry, Adrenaline Guy and Homeboy, you kind of deserve it though).

Anyway, a little more background on my experience with Tyler—I speak of him so often because yes, it was my most recent relationship, but I learned so much about life and about myself from being with this man and then ultimately, not being with him. Also, maybe I am not over it yet—get off my case and just pour me another glass of vino, damn, you nosy bitch! As you guys know, I was not perfect in this relationship. I made mistakes as I was fumbling with my self-worth and simply taking the time to grow up.

He, closer to perfect than I, struggled with opening himself up to emotional intimacy. "How you livin'?" he would ask to get a read on what I was thinking. Even though it has been months since we broke up, that line in his voice has been playing in my head all day. This echo has caused me to ponder how it might have felt to be in a relationship with me. This time not in the codependent, *OMG, what do they think of me?* way but in a more loving, curious sense.

Tyler and I dated for two and a half years. Both intensely self-aware, we fought hard to be our best selves in every moment. I already spent some time in chapter one (and throughout this entire book, actually) on my shortcomings, so if you will be so gracious, Tyler, I am going to spend a moment to lovingly discuss one of yours. I did not realize what an impact I had on this man's life until our final weekend together. Sure, he would share ways in which I helped him over the years (being a support system through hard times, being fun, loving, and understanding, blah blah) but it was not until we were both in my bed, in tears over the possibility of our relationship coming to an end, that he confessed the way his world had been changed by me.

Prior to his relationship with me, Tyler was single for three years following being cheated on by a long-term girlfriend. Similar to my experience, he was also completely damaged by his first love. That night in my room, two and a half years into our relationship, Tyler expressed to me that he used to numb his pain with marijuana every single day for the three years before he met me. I knew that he had sort of given up the habit towards when we first started dating, but I had no idea he was using it to anesthetize his natural human feelings for years. I am a legalize weed advocate, but we should always take care that we are not depending on it and getting high every minute of every day in order to escape uncomfortable feelings. Even though it is not proven to have addictive chemicals, we all know it can be a crutch—similar to social media addiction, sex, and so on.

Along with this, Tyler said he would avoid opening up to anyone, especially women. By being with me—a blabbermouth who will profess her love to you probably before it is safe to do so, he retrained himself to feel again. Tyler told me that because of the way I incautiously ran around shooting my shot at many different aspects of life, he realized that it was okay to have feelings and to give and accept love and vulnerability. This was huge for both of us. I was pretty shook up because I had no idea he was numbing his pain so severely prior to dating me. I do not bring up his testimonial to humblebrag about how incredible I am at changing men's lives. I bring it up because it nearly flipped my world upside down. I began to see myself in a new way. His anxieties around vulnerability were what caused him to take so many years to open up to me about this. The important thing is that he did (which was a big step for him as well) and for that I thank him because it was a truly pivotal moment in my journey for self-love. Better late than never, as they say!

So here I was, out there, changing lives! So much of my life I had it ingrained deep inside of me that I was the trophy girlfriend, only there for a consistent lay, a great batch of cookies, or sometimes even a shoulder to lean on if my guy wanted it. I was not fully aware of everything else that I brought to the table. Tyler encouraged me to place more worth on other aspects of myself, but the concept did not truly start to take flight until recently. After our relationship ended, I spent a lot of time alone. I let it marinate on my soul what I had done for this man and for his future relationships. I smile picturing all the ways we helped each other. It is a beautiful thing when two people who are consistently looking inward come together and share their findings. I am better because of him and he is better because of me.

Single and Ready to Mingle

I am also doing amazing out here on my own, you guys. Getting through heartbreak strengthens your relationships with friends, family, and most intensely, your relationship with yourself. I held myself when I cried and pulled myself out of bed when it felt impossible. I took this breakup like a tequila shot with a slice of lime and a grain of salt and as the opportunist I am, used it to make me better. Trust me, I have spent plenty of time lingering on what I have done wrong in all my relationships and that is valuable information, but I would like to argue that it is almost more important to focus on what you did right. This has been a giant leap in the self-love game for me.

Breakups are so good for us, you guys. Leading up to today, every relationship I was in was filled with insecurity on my end and constant worrying about all the other incredibly hot women in the world. As I mentioned in chapter one, accepting the truth that there are a countless number of devastatingly cute babes on this earth that every guy will naturally go gaga for relieved some pressure off myself. Here is a trick I learned in therapy—I used to look around, envying particular body parts, manicures, or items of clothing on other women. I trained myself to challenge this jealousy with envisioning how I would feel if I met me for the first time. I love watching candid videos of myself because I am a narcissist but also because it provides a true glimpse at what other people see when they are with me. I am pretty sure if I walked by me on the street, I would have a girl crush immediately. So why do I build up other women but then tear myself down because I do not have Kim Kardashian's gorgeous but unattainable booty? (No hate. Get it, girl. I might buy one too if I had the money). Try this exercise: if you did not know you and you saw you across a dimly lit bar in a striking romantic moment with a Robyn song playing in the background, what would you think? I'd wife.

I admire strong, independent women who rescue animals and do not need no man and live their lives unapologetically about who they are. Amidst all the self-reflection of the past few months, I realized I had become the woman I always looked up to. All the trials and tribulations of the last couple years birthed the goddess I always wished I was. What a treat. I have a theory that the chick you create in your mind as the ultimate badass is actually living inside of you. So, go ahead; picture the chick you admire, the chick you would one hundred percent wife if you were into that. What does she look like? Where does she live? What perfume does she wear? What does she do every day? As mentioned, mine is a single bad bitch living in a studio apartment with her rescue dog. She writes books, eats vegetables, and goes for her dreams. She is self-aware and loving. Oh wait, am I looking in a mirror?! The only thing missing from my reality is the giant snake tattoo my ideal bad bitch has down her left arm. Hmm, maybe someday.

That bad bitch you picture lives inside of you. You know how I know this? The image you produced stems from your own mind, your own subconscious, and your own desires, so there is your answer. It is already a part of you if you made it up in your own mind! So yup, I am going to start singing "He Lives In You" from the Lion King in your ear until you believe me. And trust me, I am widely talented in many areas, but singing is not my forte, so get your shit together, girl, because you do not want this.

Lucky To Be You

This is going to sound intensely vain, but by now you guys have gotten to know me a bit, so I feel comfortable saying this—I feel very lucky to be able to witness my own mind working firsthand. I am the first to hear my own jokes as they are formulated in my head. I was the first to have access to this wonderful book I wrote. I also love beholding growth, change, and the development of healthier thought patterns in my head. Try this exercise: note all of the cool ideas you have thought of and imagine yourself as a third party inside of your own head. A little crazy? Maybe, but it works. Unless you are super boring and just suck overall, in which case I cannot help you. If you are super fucking awesome like me, lo and behold! You get to *live* with that incredible person. You get to wake up in the morning and see *her*! Maybe it is just my narcissism, but I have arrived at a place in my journey for self-love where I genuinely feel so lucky to be with myself. You should feel blessed to be on this journey of life with yourself too, because at the end of the day, *you* are all you have got. Love up on her.

Dating Apps and Me

It would not be a book written by a millennial if I did not mention dating apps once or twice. When I was in a relationship in my early twenties, I was very grateful that I did not have to deal with the current trend in dating culture. You guessed it—the apps. I teased friends as they swiped through Tinder, confident that surely *I* would never have to resort to that. Nope, certainly *I* would find a plethora of eligible bachelors on my own! Cocky bitch. Rarely do I ever even leave my apartment for something other than work, so I am not sure where that logic came from. Boy, did I overestimate myself. First of all, I work in an industry primarily made up of people I try not to date, and second, I live in a lonely-as-hell, giant-ass city that is very social-media-focused. I quickly swallowed my pride after a few months of being single because the number of AA batteries I was going through was becoming an environmental hazard. So, for climate change and only for climate change, I downloaded the apps.

Now, I am incredibly picky. I have a difficult time finding people I am attracted to in person, so I am more than happy to unearth something I do not like about you by browsing through your photos. After lots of sifting and switching around to different styles of apps, I matched and conversed with a few seemingly eligible guys. I met one in person that ended up being a complete disappointment because I was not at all attracted to him. I blame myself for being selective but also blame Bumble guy for posting inaccurate photos of himself. Actually, I take that back. I blame no one because I simply was not into him and that is no one's fault; it is just nature, baby!

Anyway, it was not a horrible date. Bumble guy and I had a decent conversation (something I am apparently able to gauge pretty well through digital messages), only to part ways as friends at the end of the night. Even though the date was not a complete horror story, I was still somewhat scarred and probably not over my ex. A few months later, I was chatting with a guy from a different app and we decided to meet. I was so nervous about being disappointed again, but my therapist was probably sick of me crying over my ex and craving attention that would never come from Adrenaline Guy, so she encouraged me to get myself out there more. I would inevitably encounter some rejects, but I might be pleasantly surprised once or twice, she said. Ugh, okay, she has a PhD, so off I went.

Okay, Raya (another dating app) guy was cute, a pleasant surprise. Our first date was cinematic and honestly a great time. We looked at art, ate chocolate fondue, and drank wine. I think the wine and the DTLA skyline got to my head a little bit because by the end of the night I was feeling this guy! I was excited to see him again but later, more sober encounters forced me to face the fact that the guy I had made up in my head was not the guy that was sitting in front of me. Here is the thing I have learned with dating apps—it is normal to paint a picture of what you imagine the person is going to be like. Everything from his work ethic, mannerisms, and what his voice sounds like all blends into your perfect guy. The second time I hung out with Raya guy, I realized that even though I had met him in person already, I was ignoring all of the *real* personality traits that conflicted with the guy I conjured up in my head. After the second visit, I forced myself to confront the fact that the guy I drew did not exist. I was a little upset at myself for ignoring this reality on night one but figured no harm done since I realized the truth soon after. I was in a way grateful that I got to enjoy a fairy-tale night with my fake guy before realizing we were not actually compatible.

My takeaway here—pay attention to how you feel around someone you meet. Check in with your gut at all times! Our bodies send us signals that our minds often ignore. Do not get hung up on the portrait that is in your head; it could be damaging to both of you.

I am painfully aware that my book cannot single-handedly end the current fad that is *ghost* culture, but riddle me this. We have to stop. I get it: I am currently two dates in with that guy from Raya I made up in my head, faced with the reality that I am probably going to have to break things off with him. Now, it is true I do not owe him anything, but it seems clear that he wants to hang out again (for obvious reasons. I mean, have you met me?). It would be the easy way out to just slowly distance myself (which I already see myself doing—it is SO fun, guys!), but I must practice what I preach. In relationships, I require transparency. If you do not like me, fine. I just want to know. I detest guessing games. It is quite egotistical of us to imagine that if we let someone down easy, they will be so impossibly heartbroken that they will not be able to carry on. Nope, we will all be just fine without you. You want others to be honest and communicative about what they want from you, right? Let's grant others the same generosity.

I always feel so mature when I am able to deliver someone the frankness that I wish to receive in return. It is endlessly rewarding to be up front with one another. Trust me, the idea of confrontation makes my palms perspire just as much as the next codependent gal, so if I can find it in myself to send that uncomfortable text or have that stomach-churning conversation, you can too.

Acting on integrity is an easy way to appreciate yourself and fall more deeply in love with who you are. It is also great karma or whatever! Something about practicing what I preach really makes me go gaga for myself. I do not feel sincere after leaving an encounter feeling as though I was inauthentic. This is why I make a point to be honest and up front about where my head's at in all of my relationships. I am sure my partners appreciate it and as a result, I swoon every time I look in the mirror with the knowledge that I am my dream girl!

Self-love and Relationships

Once upon a time (or if I am being honest, like six months ago), I used to think that love and relationships were about being selfless. I was convinced that as one half of two, you needed to be unfailingly sacrificing and compromise the hell out of everything. I gathered that loving your partner so much so that their needs came before your own was a testament of beauty and romance. What I have learned is that for me right now, in my early twenties, it is more responsible to install the exact opposite behavior patterns. Now, I am not saying that this advice is for everyone. Assholes, you can plug your ears for this section and for God's sake just let your significant other pick the damn movie for once. Codependents, listen up. Mama is talkin' to you!

Dating men recently has been a fun way of falling in love with myself. I slay these dates! I find myself laughing at all of the charming, witty things *I* said days after a romantic evening with a new guy. I am well aware that I cannot live like this forever, but if you are interested in causal dating and bettering your relationship with yourself, use these new encounters as a tool! No harm done in my book! This is literally my book. What I say goes! You learn so much about yourself when interacting with others. A trick I have been using actually began as my New Year's resolution for 2019. If I fancy a guy, he is the permanent fixation of my thoughts twenty-four hours a day, seven days a week. I noticed this infatuation was dangerous when I would look up to these men who quite honestly, did not deserve this extreme level of adoration from me.

You know who does deserve my intense attention and racing thoughts? Me. My New Year's resolution this year was to catch myself while daydreaming about a guy. When I am entranced in envisioning all the qualities that make my man of interest so great, I shift my focus to myself. I force myself to meditate on the qualities I love about myself, *not* my guy. I love this rule. If you find yourself loving partners dangerously more than you love yourself. Try this.

When you finally do find yourself in a relationship, congratu-la-fuck-lations; try to find a balance for yourself. I worry so much about the emotional status of my partner that I am constantly checking up on his emotional state. I need to stop doing this. I need to tune into my own emotions more while on a date or when having sex and question whether or not I am having fun as opposed to solely worrying about the experience of the other. This book is posing as a vow to put myself first. Of course, we must be aware and empathetic with our partners, but for me, this comes without even trying so I know it will unfailingly occur organically. I am one hundred percent confident that I will not take selfishness too far; it is just not who I am.

From here on out, I refuse to alter my values regarding my friends, family, career, or my alone time when I am in my next relationship. Here I am, swearing on this. You are all my witnesses. Sometimes it seems like the minute I am really finding my groove as a single woman, I fall in love again. In a way, I am writing this book to hold myself accountable so the next time I am in a relationship, I can refer back and practice what I preach. For information's sake, I wish I had all the answers for you, guys. So badly, I wish I knew exactly how to curate a perfect, healthy, balanced relationship so I could spill the deets for you, my friends. We will have to talk again in my thirties or forties, I guess.

Self-forgiveness

You deserve it. As a crippling perfectionist, I am impossibly hard on myself in so many areas of my life. I used to dwell on rough interactions I had with strangers, stupid things that have come out of this mouth of mine, and of course, the millions of things I would do over given the opportunity. Something that helps me in those moments of regret is reflecting on what I learned from my mistakes. If it taught me a lesson on how to be better, it was worth it, and we can move on.

I also look back and try to be gracious and understanding of the girl I was in the moment of making said mistakes. I hold myself to such a high standard, but I try to also grant myself the same forgiveness I would to someone else had they made the same hiccup I did. Yes, I have been overly jealous, possessive, and manipulative in past relationships, but it was because I had some deeply rooted insecurities and trust issues because another guy did me wrong. Of course, it does not completely excuse the behavior, but I was also young and at twenty-three, I am now aware of so much more.

Developing self-awareness of your past mistakes is the first step. Evolving so that you do not make those mistakes again is the second. If you have done this, why not free yourself from the regret? There is no reason to gnaw at your fingernails over a mistake you made when you were twenty that you have since learned from and corrected. You've got this! I once read this quote on Twitter: "If you ever find yourself cringing at something you did in the past, it means you have grown as a person." Trust me, I am right there with you. I cringe while proofreading most of this book. It's essentially a diary of self-forgiveness and development.

Boundaries

I don't really know what these are, but I am going to try to write about them because I need to. In order to recover from codependency, I need to learn how to establish boundaries, especially in romantic relationships. Oftentimes I am drawn to men who are broken, unaware of where their distress is coming from, and in need of therapy. Coincidentally, these men are also drawn to me. Fun stuff.

I was recently on the phone with one of my besties, catching her up on a recent grievance over a man who inserted himself into my life way too quickly after being dumped by a long-term girlfriend. "I wish he'd just communicate with me and tell me what he was going through rather than being so dodgy! Tell me you're going through it, dude. Cry to me about your ex! I don't care, let's just talk about it!" I barked over my speakerphone to my girlfriend Lindsey as I drove up the 101.

That last sentence I blurted out of frustration stopped me in my tracks. Record scratch! Epiphany moment! I realized that I often pass up my lack of boundaries as being "cool" and open and honest when in reality, that behavior is simply enabling people to dump their shit on me. I am dope and blunt and all those lovely things, but it is urgent that I learn to draw some lines ASAP so that I do not get hurt even further. I saw this really great chart on Instagram by Courtney Burg that resonated deeply with me. It has been really helpful to me, so I have included it for you guys. Follow her blog! Some brilliant work here!

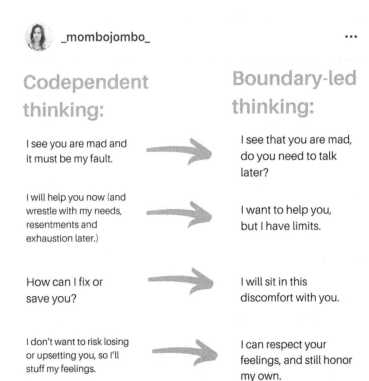

mombojombo • • •

Codependent thinking:

Boundary-led thinking:

I see you are mad and it must be my fault. → I see that you are mad, do you need to talk later?

I will help you now (and wrestle with my needs, resentments and exhaustion later.) → I want to help you, but I have limits.

How can I fix or save you? → I will sit in this discomfort with you.

I don't want to risk losing or upsetting you, so I'll stuff my feelings. → I can respect your feelings, and still honor my own.

@mombojombo

There is something tempting to me about saving people, especially men. Maybe it is the lack of control I feel over my own life at times. Maybe it is because my parents have careers in social work. Maybe it is because I grew up in the household of a recovering alcoholic. Codependency distracts us from our own issues and makes us feel validated by the feelings of another. The concept of establishing boundaries and finding a balance between my out-there humor and willingness to discuss such deep topics with others and keeping my own mental health safe is new to me. Establishing boundaries with those around us is a beautiful act of self-love and self-preservation in my opinion. Awareness is the first step, I guess. Here's to boundaries! May we know them, may we have them, may we keep them.

We Love an Inner Child Moment

I have very few vivid memories of the first grade. The American in me feels guilty that it was not 9/11, which happened that year, but a different day from that same school year. This day stands out more dramatically in my mind; the mind of a child is a complicated thing. My first-grade classroom seemed so big. It had a lot of windows and an overall bluish gray, sterile hue. This particular day, I was sitting around a table with my peers, likely working on a project. At some point, a classmate on my left-hand side removed his sweatshirt, probably because the day began to warm up as they often start off so chilly in upstate New York. If I am remembering correctly, once he took off his sweatshirt, a fun T-shirt that he bore underneath was revealed.

As a child, I was a follower. Even today, I like to look around me and observe the actions of others. Thankfully, in adulthood, I have developed the self-confidence that prevents that sometimes toxic, intrinsic magnetism to do as those around me are. At five years old, I saw my friend shed a layer of clothing and in that moment, I felt inclined to do the same. Maybe I was hot too. Maybe I liked his T-shirt. I can't remember why, but I wanted to mimic the action so badly.

I was wearing a green overshirt, the color of pine needles. It was that hybrid between a long-sleeved T-shirt and a crew-neck sweater—thinner than fleece but heavier than your standard tee. It had a screen-printed design of cats and flowers on the front. I really liked it. Underneath I had on one of those little camisoles that come in packets of three, rolled up into a tiny, shiny plastic bag made by Hanes or whatever. Do they still sell those? I'd get the pastel ones that included a white one, a baby pink one, and a powder blue. That day I was wearing my favorite, the pink one. Duh.

Sitting there at that table in class, I removed my forest-green overshirt, leaving me in my camisole. I can't remember how I got there but the next thing I knew, I was in the coat closet in the back of the classroom with my teacher. She was a thin middle-aged woman with a weird triangle haircut that should have been left in the eighties. She was bent forward, and I can still see her bony finger being waved in my face as we were surrounded on all sides by colorful backpacks. My parents were never aggressive in-your-face scolders so that could be part of the reason I have such a strong recollection of this moment. "Put your shirt back on this instant!" she spewed in a harsh tone. "Some people consider what you're wearing to be UNDERWEAR!" She really emphasized the word *underwear.*

What happened following the closet scold, I am not entirely sure. I don't know if I cried. I am sure I did not argue back. My age and untouchable trust in authority immediately caused me to blame myself even though I was thoroughly confused. I did not realize I had done something wrong. I knew not to get naked at school, so what was the problem? She was my teacher though, so in my mind, she had to be right. At five years old, I did not have the cognitive ability to question that. This is why we have to be so careful with the way we treat children. Our words and our actions get absorbed into their tiny bodies. When they see Mommy and Daddy fighting over who will take them to soccer practice, they automatically assume fault. Their world is too simple for children to think of any other reason for the conflict. I carried out an action and as a result, my teacher got heated and angry. It was my fault.

There are obviously so many better ways my first-grade teacher could have handled this incident. The twenty-three-year-old me is frustrated with this situation for a number of reasons that are also obvious. I won't get too far into all of it, but come on, a five-year-old in a tank top is really a problem?! No, society is the problem. Let's stop shaming children when adults are the ones having sick thoughts. Would a child who was a boy have been treated the same way I was had he taken his shirt entirely off? Probably not. Okay, sorry, I just really had to get that one off my chest.

I was made to feel ashamed of my body at age five. I was threateningly instructed by someone I respected that my body needed to be covered, told that it was inappropriate to show even if only for my own comfort. During a crucial age of development, I felt embarrassed of my body and as though my presence was inconvenient and disturbing to others. In childhood, we should be learning about all of the wonderful things our bodies are capable of. We should be learning how to cherish them as a vessel for our souls, and as tools we can use to communicate to those around us. Obviously, children should also know not to strip down in public, but you get my point here, right? Looking back on this incident, I suspect that it may have stunted my instillation of self-love. I learned guilt and insecurity that day. Those emotions feel the exact opposite way self-love should.

I was brought back to this memory recently after completely shutting it out of my mind forever. I was sitting beside a very sweet mother and a daughter. Mom gently instructed her eight-year-old daughter that if she became too warm, she could take off her sweatshirt. BOOM, instantly I was not sitting in that waiting-room chair but was back in that coat closet of my first-grade classroom. A tightness formed in my chest; my present-day world began to circle; my vision grew blurry; and I suddenly became emotional and concluded that maybe this event impacted me more than I realized. It certainly seems that way since I damn near cried when a mother offered her daughter the lovely gesture of ownership over her own body. I felt happy for this young girl and her mother while simultaneously feeling pity and helplessness for five-year-old me.

A therapist or hypnotist might say this event that occurred when I was so young contributed to my hypersensitivity to those around me and how the way I am acting affects them. A professional might also say that being scolded for revealing my shoulders taught me to be ashamed of my body. I may worry that my presence is inconvenient and brings discomfort to others. I do constantly look to others for verbal reassurance, so I don't know, maybe it is my inner child desperately begging for approval and forgiveness.

What I do know is this: little moments from our childhoods do affect us as adults. It is sometimes fun to play detective and try to analyze why we are the way that we are. What is more important, though, is to figure out how to reverse these patterns that were subconsciously branded to our brains when they were in an early stage of development. I have made it a point, and still do, to fight off that insecure, follow-the-leader little girl that lives inside of me. In chapter three I told you how watching a video of myself at three years old made me realize it was time to learn how to recover from my eating disorder. I picture that girl's innocence whenever I am tempted to skip dinner. I visualize embracing her in a hug and telling her it's not her fault when I remember her taking on too much responsibility for the happiness of those around her. Inner-child work is Therapy 101 and for good reason. We would never starve, withhold forgiveness from, or tell a toddler that she is unworthy of love or happiness, so treat yourself with the same respect. As I have gone over in this chapter, it has taken many, many years to truly understand my value and know that I have a strong, powerful place in this world. Do it for your inner child, y'all!

Not Giving a Fuck

You know how people always talk about how aging is great because you begin to give fewer and fewer fucks as time goes by? Especially about silly things like how others perceive you? People always tease me when I declare my excitement about being fifty someday. I know, I know, I will not wish my twenties away; the whirlwind of learning shit about myself and being broke has been completely cathartic and rewarding. I am trying to stay present and enjoy my stupidity, *but* I do look forward to that solid-as-a-rock self-love so much that I have been fighting to cheat time and expedite the process. I have noticed that not giving a fuck what others think of you really does only come with time, but if we are self-aware and dedicated to the art of relieving ourselves from self-consciousness, we can create a significantly happier life for ourselves.

We all know those people who seem so insecure it makes us uncomfortable. I have witnessed people (usually women) gawk around themselves in fear and attempt to hide in every room they enter. There could be other issues that contribute to their constant panic but sometimes I just wanna smack 'em! And I am pretty sensitive and understanding! I just want to be like, *girl, no one gives a FUCK about what you are wearing or what you are doing.* It is a harsh reality, but it is true. As long as you are a good person, anyone who thinks ill of you is straight-up wrong and it becomes a reflection of them, so there ya go; responsibility falls from your hands. Carry on with your day mighty fine!

As women, there are an infinite number of elements society tries to convince us that we should be insecure about. We must rise above. Catering to anyone's wishes but our own is a damn waste of time. I am a firm believer that you can work on improving the parts of yourself you want to while simultaneously loving yourself tremendously. We all look up to people who are unapologetically and authentically themselves, so if you truly want people to think you are a badass, fake it until you make it!

Obviously, the opinions of those we love and respect matter to us. I am not saying you need to be so reckless that you become toxic to the people around you. I am talking about general self-consciousness, especially focusing on the opinions of people who do not mean anything to you. You are never going to please everyone. Someone is always going to disagree with the way you live, so, girl, do what makes *you* happy. There is nothing more freeing than releasing a book about all my flaws and truly not giving a fuck if you guys think I am crazy. I think I am awesome, and I love who I am. Discovering this deep amount of self-love and acceptance is helping me on my way to becoming less of a people pleaser in jobs, friendships, and relationships. Love yourself, chica. You are all you got! The sooner you do this, the healthier all of your relationships will become.

Goodbye, haters! I will only shave my legs when *I* want to feel like a silky-smooth mermaid goddess. Good riddance to the parts of me that are desperate for male approval. See ya in my next relationship, probably! (Just kidding, guys. I promise I will try.)

Chapter Eight

We Love the 405

"So what are you going to do with a BFA in dance?" If I had a dollar for every time someone asked me that question in college, I could have bought shots for everyone at Slick Willie's Sports Bar every Thursday night for four years. When I was seventeen, I decided to audition for the dance programs at a few reputable colleges. My parents said, "All right, sweetie, if that is what you want," because they are angels and drove me all around the northeast to visit some options.

I was not exactly sure what I wanted to do when I grew up, like so many students my age. No subjects in school interested me as much as I loved racing to dance class every day the minute the bell rang. There was an alumna from the dance studio I attended growing up who was four or five years older than me and had attended the University at Buffalo and majored in dance. One of my most idolized teachers at that studio also graduated from the program. Go to ballet every morning instead of math class?! Sign me right up, thank you very much!

While immersed in the program, I was exposed to the overwhelming number of options offered in the field of professional dance. Concert-style companies would come in and teach master classes when they were in town. What a dream, I thought, to be dancing all day, performing around the country, and that is your job?! Wow!

I had a number of peers who were interested in teaching younger generations and dedicated their time to educating themselves in order to become great educators for the future. There is also the scienc-y side of dance that interested some of my classmates. They took more medically focused classes, and some would later join the physical therapy program at the university. A few minored in health and wellness and produced exceptional projects on nutrition and leading a healthy lifestyle.

When I attended Buffalo, I FaceTimed my boyfriend too frequently, spent far too much time on the elliptical, and had a crush on my writing professor (if only either of us knew I'd write a book someday!). Maybe I should have taken the time to consider minoring in writing or psychology (which I also took a semester of) but at the time, I was only interested in dance performance, so I went ahead and pursued the single major in dance, on track to get my bachelor of fine arts degree. *Only* majoring in dance and focusing on the performance aspect is completely respectable and I think it was a great choice for me considering I made it at such a young age.

Even within a focus on dance performance, there are numerous paths one can go down. Most of the people I know who went to college for dance performance ended up moving to New York City, Los Angeles, or worked a traveling job such as a national tour or a cruise ship. Or they got married. Hey, I am not knocking it. These are just the facts. You do you, boo. While in school, I learned that Los Angeles was more central for commercial dance-focused jobs and seemed to be a better fit for me based on recommendations from peers and professors. And the idea of LA sounded very romantic to me. What an exciting place! I could live near the beach, get out of Upstate

New York winters, and live my dreams? Get me that one-way ticket already; I was ready for my Miley moment!

I followed in the footsteps of a couple dancers one and two years ahead of me who had visited Los Angeles in their time off over the summers. So, I spent two weeks in LA during the summer before my junior year of college and then again the summer before my senior year so I could test it out and dip my feet into the chilly Pacific waters. I enrolled in some training programs at the professional dance studios there and worked my little behind off every day, surrounded by the best dancers in the world. Holy shit, it was intimidating. I remember being overwhelmed, self-conscious, and a little bit lost in most of the classes, but despite all of that, I fought my hardest and managed to adapt to my surroundings and somehow not get swallowed whole.

My second summer in LA I attended an open-call audition for a dance agency. I had been through auditions before for college and whatnot, but this was my first one in the real world. There were probably three hundred dancers in that giant gray warehouse with poor air conditioning. I had only found out about the audition a few days before. My friend whose futon I was crashing on told me she was going and that I should too, just for the experience. So, in true LA fashion, at the last minute, I printed a shitty headshot at a local Walgreens, put on some lipstick, and did my very best to pick up the challenging hip-hop choreography that, at nineteen, I definitely lacked the swag to do any justice.

I remember being surrounded by sweaty bodies that were clothed in way cooler outfits than I. I peered through the crowd to try and see the dance I was about to perform in front of complete strangers in mere minutes. I felt all right about the audition. I picked up the steps to the best of my ability and am pretty sure I did not completely embarrass myself. Of course, they did not call me and offer me a spot. I swear auditions can give us low-key PTSD. My heart still races with anxiety when I hear "Dessert" by Dawin.

The time I spent in LA in the summers was exhausting and intimidating. I found ways to have fun on my days off, but I definitely was not in love with the place. During each visit, I was always eager to head back home. Career-wise, though, I knew it was where I needed to be. I did not move to Los Angeles because I liked it. To be quite honest, I actually did *not* like it for a long time. I moved here because I loved dance and I wanted to make it my job.

I graduated college a semester early in December 2016. About two months later, I permanently relocated to Los Angeles, leaving my family, friends, familiarity, and a man I loved dearly. I started out with a roommate in a two-bedroom apartment in Studio City. That year was by far the most difficult of my life. I had one or two friends I knew from UB who'd graduated a few years ahead of me and lived out here. They would meet me for the occasional coffee or invite me out with them, but that was about it. They were busy with their own lives and did not have time for my unemployed, clueless ass.

I totally get it. I am them now. In a desperate attempt for money, stability, and routine, I hunted for a part-time job that would keep me afloat and I got into dance classes. I had a friend who did some modeling so she showed me a site where I could meet up with photographers and build my portfolio to get some good content. I adjusted to my dramatic life change by filling my lonely days with photo shoots with strangers, (something I could never do now, yikes), dance classes, and random brand-ambassador jobs where I would get paid to hand out free Coca Cola. I even sat in the audience of some TV shows for some extra cash.

In my time here, I have learned that the path of following your dreams is full of many things. Most prominent and essential, I would like to argue, is the ability to accept change, surrender control, and adapt to your environment. Let me tell you, it is not for the faint of heart. I am still not entirely sure how I survived those first six months before two of my good friends from my graduating class moved into my apartment building that fall. I pretty much went insane. I knew a bit about the dance industry and that my goal was to get signed by an agency, so I went to every open call I heard of, worked sporadic gigs, kept training, and found myself a good therapist.

I initially left Tyler behind in Buffalo, but we decided to take a whack at a long-distance relationship, so I spent time planning our trips, talking on the phone with him, and keeping in close contact with my best friends who also lived far away. When Cait and Alissa moved across the hall, life slowly started to get better.

At this point, I had developed an anxiety disorder (more on this in chapter ten), so in-person friends were a really great idea. I had now found a groove, working part-time at a boutique weight-lifting fitness studio, and once a week doing a work-study program at an elite local dance studio. I had made some casual dance acquaintances at work, class, and auditions. Eventually, a few of these relationships developed and I was asked to be in some local live dance shows. They were unpaid projects where dancers could exercise their choreography tools and showcase their work. It is a necessary step we all take here; a vetting process of performing for free around town.

The ball was rolling in the right direction. For me, it was a very slow-moving ball. I am shy (this might come as a surprise to you since you are likely a complete stranger and I have let you in on all of my most personal struggles) with the outside world and it feels unnatural for me to kiss the asses of those who are higher than me in the industry. By staying true to what feels natural and ethical to me, my ball has moved slowly, but my integrity is something I am immensely proud of.

After I hit my one-year anniversary of living in LA, I did some serious reflecting on the previous year and made a plan to refocus my path to ensure I got signed by an agent in 2018. I put myself out there more than I had in the previous year. I opened my eyes to the professional relationships I had already been curating organically. I worked harder and I simply kept pushing onward. Open-agency calls like the one I attended the previous summer were getting more packed every time one was held. There were sometimes up to five hundred hopeful dancers, but I still attended unfailingly and performed to the best of my ability. I invested more time in professional relationships because the open calls were such a nightmare that I was nearly convinced that I was not going to get noticed at one.

Another key I've found on the path to success is that the adaptation process never ends. You do not adjust your perspective once and then are home free. You must practice a constant cycle of adapting over and over again, especially in a city as fast-moving as Los Angeles. Here, we meet resiliency. Resiliency is the time and continuous, never-ending effort you put into your work. Resiliency is the willingness to adapt over and over again. Resiliency is moving forward through change and continually adding building blocks to your foundation.

Embracing this concept of resiliency, I enrolled in a training program with one of the best heels teachers in our industry in the summer of 2018. Yes, dancing in four-inch stilettos is a requirement for female professional dancers. Dancing in high heels is a whole new ballgame so we take extra time to properly train in them. "Heels" is even now considered a style and genre of dance that can incorporate elements from other styles like jazz, hip-hop, and contemporary. I learned a lot from my teacher in those four weeks, but I instantly took away some ideas as to why I did not stand out in auditions despite the things I thought I was doing right. I realized I was fading into the background and I was not dancing like I wanted to be seen. A month later I attended an open call with one of the dance agents. I had been cut from this agent's auditions *three* times before over the past year and a half.

On that October morning, I danced like I wanted to be seen. Not for nothing, but Tyler and I had broken up the night before this open call. I went in because I hold myself accountable for that type of shit. You guys should, too. Do not sell yourself short. Even if you think you will not be chosen out of a room of five hundred mascaraed dancers, take the damn risk and fight for that spot.

That is exactly what I did that Saturday in early October 2018. I looked cute, danced hard, and carried myself with poise and ease. I stood where I could be seen and made eye contact with the agents. They kept me through multiple cuts all the way through the end. This had never happened for me at one of these open calls before. There were probably twenty of us at the end and they collected our headshots and resumes. They said they would call us if we were selected. I was astounded and I felt a great sense of accomplishment. I was confident that they wanted me and was completely impressed with my resilience and defiance and the overall way I slayed! I had earned this.

I had been having good auditions for years and learned from each one. My hard work showed. A few days later, I opened an email from the Movement Talent Agency congratulating me on my offer to sign with them. I cried on my bedroom floor and called my parents and friends. This was a huge step. A few weeks before that audition, I had booked my first big dance job with a choreographer I had been taking classes from by simply showing up, bringing my best, and being myself. All of a sudden, I was doing what I came to LA to do.

Now, I understand this success in my story only took a few pages to draw out, but that does not do justice to all of the hard work I had to put forth. I cannot stress enough how deeply I had to dig into myself to accomplish this goal and how many long days filled with failure it took me to get to where I am now. Do not be discouraged. All you can do is keep going. Remember, resiliency.

So, I have accomplished some previous career goals of mine, and now there are new ones in their place. I am doing the LA dancer thing that once seemed so far out of my reach. My agent sends me on auditions nearly every week. I work part-time jobs to keep food on my table and in my dog's dish. I take classes and constantly train to be better. When I am on a dance job, it is heaven. It makes me look forward to more that are yet to come. On certain days where I am not booking work, it feels like I will never work again. Getting cut from auditions repeatedly is part of the game. Having your agent call you and let you know that you should clear your schedule because the casting office has you in their final choices for the role, only to have them go with someone else, fucking sucks.

I've been ghosted by more casting directors than I have romantic partners! I like to take time to appreciate how far I have come, but I will admit that it is so hard when you still feel as though you have so far to go. My goal is longevity. I know that if I keep working hard and practicing adaptation while remaining resilient, I will someday book those enviable dance jobs. I am here to stay, baby.

"So, what are you going to do with a BFA in dance?" they would all ask, most with the best of intentions. I would smile and reply with something about commercial dance in LA and how *yeah, you just get an agent and they send you on auditions* and so on. I told the story of my dreams as if they were a distant fairy tale; that is what they felt like at the time. I was never the best dancer in my group in high school and college surrounded me with even more incredible talent. This was a beneficial element for me because it always kept me humble and it made me better since I rose to the talent level of my peers rather than getting comfortable.

I remember answering people's questions about my chosen career aspirations with doubt in the back of my mind. I knew being a professional dancer was a thing, but I honestly was not sure I was talented enough to do it. But here I am, doing it. I came to this place and did something I never thought I could do. I am here to tell you to believe in your wildest dreams. You can be a professional artist. Your celebrity crush could send you a direct message on Instagram asking for your phone number. You can live the life you never imagined. I promise nothing is impossible. Onward and upwards we go.

Los Angeles has wiggled its way into this heart of mine. I come from such a fun-loving part of the country, full of neighborhood families, made up of unwavering love and humility for their sports teams, and staples of fried food. Being around so much plastic surgery and people who are married to their careers and their images was a culture shock for me. I am so glad I gave it time, though. Sure, there are douchebags here and you run into a lot of people you know immediately that you do *not* want to be friends with, but I must say I have met some pretty incredible people out here, too. For every snooty person, there is someone else who looks you in the eye, asks how your day was, and you can feel that they genuinely care.

I have found a support system in the clientele at the gym where I work. A lot of them have kids my age and they check in on what is going on in my life and let me know they have my back if I ever need it. These are middle-aged, successful people who I only met a year or two ago! They have absolutely nothing to gain from the front-desk worker who checks them in at their gym, but they are good fucking people. I feel the same way about a lot of the people I work for. I am constantly in awe of the characters I encounter in the dance community. Most of the dancers I have crossed paths with are extremely supportive. Yes, they are out here fighting for their dreams too, but we have all been through the struggle. So in a way, we all have each other's backs.

I have a Buffalo family here now. It started when Cait and Alissa moved here, and it just keeps multiplying and getting larger. I have a group of now six or seven of us that all went to school together. We go to movies, giggle at Netflix, cry together on hard days, and dance nights away at clubs in West Hollywood. We take our best shot at cooking Thanksgiving dinners and take little road trips to nearby cities. I am so incredibly thankful for them. This local support system has become crucial to my well-being. I trust these people with my life, and my dog when I go out of town, so yeah, my life. This family has curated this crazy-huge city into a home for me.

This town has put me through it, though. Here I have experienced infinite rejection and too many sad, lonely days to count. This place initially represented heartbreak to me but now it also represents healing because of all the work I have done on myself. You heard me: *I* did that work, no one else! Self-work is not easy. Pursuing a career as an artist is not easy. Breakups are not easy. Moving is not easy and this city certainly will not hand you anything on a silver platter. Los Angeles is not exactly an effortless place to be happy despite all of the flower crowns, CBD smoothies, and sunshine. It can be a lonely, devastating town if you let it. But if you search deep down inside of yourself for love, it will manifest in the world that surrounds you.

I have impressed myself with my adaptability and resiliency over the past couple years. I have more strength than I ever thought I did and now LA is symbolic of that. I am a sentimental person so this environment that shaped me and grew me now holds a colossal place in my heart. I used to scoff at the traffic, fake boobs, and angel-wing murals painted everywhere, but now these are just characteristics of my favorite city on Earth.

Sometimes I roll my windows down, blast my Spotify playlist titled "Cali"—with all LA songs on it, of course—and I soak it all in. I gaze around at the giant mountains and palm trees with adoration. When I take a day to be a tourist in my own city, you can find me sniffling, choked up with love on the Venice boardwalk, dumbfounded by the beauty of the Pacific. I love you, California. Thank you, Los Angeles, for chewing me up, spitting me out, stomping on me with your red-bottom heels, and ultimately making me a better person. I hope you do not break off into the ocean any time soon due to climate change. Xoxo.

Los Angeles also brought me my furry companion, whom you may have seen star in all of my Instagram stories. I was twenty-two years old when I decided I could not go another day without a dog clicking her little paws around my home. I had spent numerous nights crying on websites of local rescue organizations, wishing I could single-handedly solve the homeless dog crisis and in return earn daily loving kisses from one or sixteen of my very own adopted pets.

Growing up, my parents always rescued dogs. I went with them to the animal shelters and later to dog-training classes and frequent visits to the park and the vet's office. I thought I had a grasp on dog-owner life and all it took was a $25 adoption sale from a local shelter I had my eye on (Best Friend's Animal Society—they are amazing) and the approval from my two roommates at the time and next thing I knew, I was zooming down the 405 to the NKLA shelter.

I visited for the first time, knowing I could not bring home a friend that day as I had a few more loose ends to tie up. My girlfriend Cait and I walked down the aisles, teary-eyed, melting over the sweet babies who were available for adoption. I got a head start on some paperwork and took down information about a couple pitties I was interested in. A few days later, after keeping an eye on the website, I headed back by myself to meet the dogs I was interested in. I had noticed a new beauty on the website, a five-year-old caramel-colored mutt they temporarily named Cappuccino. Her goofy grin in the shot on the website pulled me in immediately. I had to meet her.

When I pulled into the shelter that sunny day, Billy Joel's "Lullaby (Goodnight, My Angel)" was playing on the radio. I told the staff that I was interested in meeting Cappuccino. She entered the yellow greeting room on a mission, nose down, sniffing the floor, desk, and couch. She was full of energy as she paced around and eventually discovered me sitting there and greeted me with a few licks. She was a sweetie and we got along right away. I could tell she had a lot on her mind by the way she was constantly scanning the area. Her ribs were visible at first glance; she had been rescued as a stray a few months prior. The shelter had spayed her and helped her put on some weight in the interim. I was instantly amused by her buoyant personality. She was the one for me.

They brought her back into her holding room while I paid and filled out some more paperwork. I was nervous and began to grow overwhelmed with the amount of responsibility that I was about to take on. I waited by the doors for the tattooed, very cute by the way, attendant to bring my dog to me. I could see them through the glass as he rounded the corner with her. I instantly began to cry. I felt like I was in one of those viral YouTube clips of a groom tearing up as his bride walks down the aisle. Except it was me overcome with emotion seeing my new dog walk towards me accompanied by the cute male staff member (call me), tugging on the leash.

I renamed my girl Pinot after one of my favorite wine grapes. Noir being a steady favorite and Grigio, an occasional beloved treat during the summertime. Sort of cliché for a twenty-two-year-old white girl to name her first dog after her favorite wine, but hey, I am only human. Best Friend Animal Society's professionals estimated that Pinot was about five years old when I adopted her. Other than her being found as an underweight, unspayed stray, they did not know anything about her history. This is typically the case with rescues, so it is essential to take extra care when getting to know them. I did so much reading prior to adoption and I thought I knew a lot going into this because I was raised with rescues.

They estimated that she is a German Shepherd and rottweiler mix, but her adorably droopy face suggests some sort of boxer and her goofy grin and bow legs may suggest some terrier as well. Who knows! What we do know is those wrinkles on her forehead are to DIE FOR. Pinot is now about sixty-five pounds of squeaky dorkiness.

Pinot's dominant personality revealed itself right away with her leash pulling and territory scanning. I knew I was going to need some help with all of this, so we signed up for some adult training classes at a local pet store. My time with Pinot started out very stressful; it was difficult to walk her because of the tugging, so I was running back and forth to the store to try out different collars and harnesses that would make walks even manageable. She is a big dog and for her, no exercise is too much exercise.

I will not lie to you: I definitely made countless mistakes with her training. My friend who is a dog trainer says some of the owners she works with who are the biggest assholes tend to be the best dog trainers. I, at the time, was an anxious mess, causing my dog to be an anxious mess. Come on, I thought, she was supposed to be *my* emotional support animal not the other way around! Anyway, I learned a lot of things the hard way. Emotions travel through a leash, so I quickly had to get my shit together in order to be a competent leader. Still to this day, I sometimes stop us on our walks to just breathe so I can transfer calm energy to her.

Again, I do not know Pinot's background, but it is evident that she was either separated from her mother too young or just never socialized with other dogs. Our training sessions were loud and migraine-inducing. Most of the work our trainer had us do was to simply get her to look at other dogs without freaking out. Looking back, I am sure my fear of potential incidents with the other animals just increased her fear of them. Her anxiety desperately called for me to calm the fuck down because her doggy brain does not have the logic that my human brain does so I had to be the one to get their shit together if this was ever going to work.

I did everything I knew to try and make this dog trust me. I attempted to claim the role as alpha by always making sure

I ate meals before her, set boundaries like not allowing her on my furniture, walked through doors before her, and tried my best to not put up with her bullshit.

I was faced with the reality that rescuing a dog posed more challenges than I had anticipated. But, Mama didn't raise no quitter, so what did I do? I adapted and played to the best of my ability with the cards I had been dealt. Of course, I made a few errors, like having her sleep in bed with me our first few nights, just because I did not know what else to do. I was overcome with love and worry. Pinot is headstrong and she could sense my imperfections very early on. She took it on herself to be the guard dog of the house, constantly scanning the perimeter, and barking at any other dogs that walked by.

Back to the dog socialization classes. She obviously had had a tougher background than I had anticipated, so I adjusted my expectations of having an easygoing emotional support animal. I adapted to my circumstances and signed her up for these classes. There was another rescue, a pure German Shepherd in our class, who was very reactive, similar to Pinot. They would wail at each other from a distance for the entire hour.

One day, as instructed, I was waiting by a stack of dog food with Pinot. The trainer rounded the corner with the shepherd and we both misjudged the proximity of the dogs and they barked and lunged at each other, making brief contact only for a second before we pulled them away. It did not look bad, just like a little nose-to-nose nipping, and both dogs calmed down pretty quickly following the incident. They were across the room when we noticed some blood on the floor around the shepherd. It was dripping from a small gash on her wet black nose. She was not crying as if in pain, thank God, but I instantly started to tear up.

I could not believe my Pinot had hurt her classmate. One of my worst fears had come to fruition and the guilt was monstrous. It is hard to blame Pinot for this mistake because in all fairness, it was induced equally by both parties and it could have easily been Pinot who ended up with the nose bleed. I do not blame her for being afraid; her classmate did bare teeth every time she barked at Pinot and I guess Pinot reacted on instinct to protect herself when afraid. I wish I could just tell her that we love other dogs and should not be scared or protective. Pinot's classmate was seemingly unbothered by her small injury. I did not even hear a whimper out of her and thankfully they got the bleeding to stop pretty quickly.

Our dog trainer probably thinks I am crazy because of how hard I cried to him that day. My intention in rescuing a dog was to help the greater good of all animals. The idea that anyone would get hurt in the process broke my heart in two. Pinot's anxiety around other doggos has not improved much despite completing the course, distanced show and gos at various parks, and my improved response—I am much calmer now. We have learned to adapt, crossing the street on our walks when we see an oncoming dog, and keeping her away from windows in my house so she is not constantly barking at passersby. I cannot take her to off-leash dog parks because I do not want to risk the safety of anyone. She is not a hip sidekick who can accompany me to coffee shops, breweries, or public festivals, but she is my companion and I am all she's got, so we make do.

I point this out because I want other imperfect dog owners who bear guilt to feel less alone. As long as you are doing the best you can and learning from mistakes, it will all be okay. I also want to advise those who are considering adopting one of their own to keep in mind that dog-parent life is not just the cute videos we post on Instagram. It is expensive vet bills and embarrassing moments when your dog decides to jump on a stranger visiting your home. It is loud and messy. Taking responsibility for another living being who has her own baggage calls for constant adjustment and reevaluation of your actions. If something I originally wanted to do does not work for Pinot, I must grow more flexible, step aside, and make room for her needs, which are not stagnant or predictable. They evolve over time, just as life does.

I like to believe that Pinot is mostly a happy pup, but I feel intense guilt when she is stressed, wondering if I had done something differently early on in our relationship, would she be calmer? And yes, all you Los Angeleian hippies, we *have* tried CBD oil. I was not equipped with the knowledge on how exactly to deal with a dog of her possible background when I initially adopted her, but everyone turned out okay, so maybe, in fact, I was. I sometimes wonder if she would be happier in a different home, with someone more experienced and with more money than me to buy her a million toys or a backyard.

I think the guilt of being a bad parent occurs to anyone who has children, human or not, from time to time. I ponder if my crazy schedule and unpredictable lifestyle has taken a toll on her. What pulls me back to earth is the faith that she seems to love me just as much as I love her.

I do not know what happened in her life before she met me. A lot can go wrong in five years and she has undoubtedly been through some dramatic changes in that time. When I adopted her, I vowed to be the constant in her life—someone who would never leave her, as Billy Joel promises in his "Lullaby." No matter how many times we have had to pack up and move; I have had to dip into my savings account for her vet bills; I have been forced to leave for a long day of work, or trust her with friends while I go out of town; she will always have me. That seems to be enough. Maybe I was in over my head bringing another life filled with its own complications and demons into my already messy one.

But it's true her difficulties shaped me into a more empathetic person and my experience with her has strengthened my ability to adapt and practice resilience.

What my Pinot has also taught me is that I am not perfect. I never will be, but I have earned her love anyway. She has also shown me that she is not perfect, either, but I am still capable of loving her wholly and unconditionally anyway.

Despite her inability to socialize with other dogs, Pinot is spectacular with other humans and that is such a gift. She will give you kisses within seconds of knowing you. She will make happy little pig snorts if you scratch her ears and she will steal your heart before you can even escape her strong wagging-tail whips. There is something magical about her. I know she is my dog, so of course I am saying this, but ask anyone in their right mind who has met her (yes, people who do not like dogs are not in their right minds). She is loving, therapeutic, and goofy. She makes me laugh and fills my heart with love. She is your favorite rom-com in dog form. Being around her is inspirational. I aim to live my life in the unapologetic fashion she does—carefree of your opinion on her loud farts, snoring, and the moaning grumbles she makes as she scarfs down her food.

My Pinot, also known as PP, my lovechild, baby, hunni, buttercup, peanut butter cup, caramel chocolate peanut butter cup, P, Peen, and so on, has made me a more patient person. She has taught me about true sacrifice and unconditional love. I have learned massive lessons from the errors I made in her training and still try my best every day to make her better and happier. I learned how to stretch my ability to adapt even further than I could have ever imagined. Of course, the thought of a day without her seems unbearable, but it does bring me some relief and I am able to cut myself a break knowing that she is my first dog of my very own and there will certainly be more. Because of my experiences with her, I will now be better equipped for future rescue dogs. Just like boyfriends!

There are some days in my life when I do not have an exciting dance gig or even anything to look forward to. These days sometimes seem impossible to face and prior to her, I would not get out of bed and eventually think myself into a depression, but she does not let that happen. The simplicity of her needing breakfast and a walk gives my life meaning when all other purpose has slipped. Our long morning strolls have turned into a meditation for both of us. I put in my headphones, hit play on an album, podcast, or audiobook, and we just go under the Los Angeles sun. It is heavenly. Fear creeps in about my incompetence or about a dance job I may or may not book, but I keep in mind that we will always have each other in one way or another and therefore we will always be okay.

I do not know what I would be without her. Who else would I sing terribly to and dance around the house with? Who else would I sit on the floor and rest my head on? She does this adorable thing where when I sit on the ground and face her, she rests her head on my shoulder. We just sit there and nuzzle into each other's necks. I cherish our little moments together and I think she does too. It is completely healing to have a furry friend follow you around your studio apartment looking up at you as if you are God just because you can reach the cupboard where her food is. Fuck, I just had to write a section about my dog; now there are no more tissues in Los Angeles.

She cannot read the dedication I made to her in this book; she cannot see all the likes she gets on my Instagram page; and she cannot understand the English sentence "you changed my life," but I think she knows. Adopt, don't shop, y'all. It will make you better. And it will make this world better.

Chapter Nine

At Least I Don't Look As Shitty As I Feel

Hey, you. Stop lying to people. The world is not going to end if you just ask someone for some goddamn help. Although accomplishing tasks on my own fills me with a sense of pride, you can definitely find me cursing myself out while sweating bullets trying to move myself into a new apartment with exactly zero help or spending my life savings on a dog sitter because I am too afraid to ask my friends to watch Pinot again. I may have had you guys fooled, ya know, with all of the totally respectable choices I have made over the years, but shocker, I am not superwoman. I am fiercely independent, but I also need assistance from time to time. We all do. Life is too long and burdensome to do all on your own and you definitely cannot carry that mattress to your car by yourself, trust me.

I am tirelessly committed to softening the burden of my existence on others. This, my dear friends, is a damaging habit because once I do finally break down and require assistance, I have trouble asking for it. If I feel as though I am inconveniencing someone, I immediately begin to panic and sweat. If I want to go to a live show because they make me happy, I tell my friends I will buy them drinks if they come with me. Typically, they react with something like, "No, what the hell?! I want to go!" Music to my ears. When I got a dog, every time she would bark in the house my stomach would drop and I would panic that I was disturbing my roommates even though they had agreed to welcome her into our home.

I also have an issue with protecting people from my pain and my emotions. While on the endlessly failing feat of trying to make the lives of those around me as physically easy as possible, I also mask disturbances I am feeling inside for the sake of their comfort. I am not sure exactly where in my conditioning I was taught that I was an annoying, bothersome piece of shit who does not deserve the love, care, and attention of those around me, but here I am, trying to get better about all of this. My early twenties sound like a great time to get started on breaking this habit. From here on out, I would like to be more transparent and less codependent. I find it to be a mature and admirable quality to have the ability to take a big giant swallow of all of that pride you've got and let yourself be seen as a human being with flaws, shortcomings, and needs.

The first thing my therapist asks me when I sit down on her gray couch is, "How are you?"

"Good," I always answer, regardless of the number of tears we both know I am going to be spewing and the alarming number of her tissues I will be soiling within the next fifty minutes. I once heard someone declare that if you reply to a formality like "How are you?" with anything other than "Good, thanks," you are a jackass. I agree to some extent. You definitely should not be sobbing about your breakup to your Trader Joe's cashier, but I worry we carry this over into our personal interactions with people who care deeply about our well-being. I sure do. I do it with my fucking therapist who I am *paying* to tell just how *not okay* I am. Why do I do this? I think a lot of it is because of that inner-child drama and the way I was raised to care for others.

Addressing feelings is messy, painful, and complicated so sometimes it is easier to avoid talking about them altogether. Sometimes your feelings do, in fact, hurt other people. I have discussed this subject with my therapist quite a bit. She insists that the feelings I worry will disturb others are feelings that everyone has and needs to express. We need to accept that our existence simply and incontrovertibly affects others. And it should. I try my best to be there for my friends when they need me. I even get a ton of emotional satisfaction from it. She reminds me that those who are close to me would feel the same sense of warmth when helping me as I do with them.

We all love stepping in to help a stranger, right? I know I do. Unless it's 4 in the morning and you are an old couple asking me how to use the very self-explanatory check-in kiosk at the airport. So, from now on, I am going to try to see my moments of need not only as times to seek self-benefit, but also as opportunities to grant the satisfaction of true intimacy with those around me. You should too!

Ankle Sprains, Ugh

I was not sure where I was going to place my struggle with chronic ankle sprains in this book. Masochism, maybe? Possibly the health is wealth chapter (10), later on? It fits here in the *stop protecting people from your pain* chapter because this more recent incident opened my eyes up to some underlying mental issues I have been dealing with alongside these pesky sprains. I tend to dismiss their severity and frequency. I write them off to others as no big deal because they are so common and embarrassing. I don't want people worrying about my physical or mental issues. But, here I go, I'm going to talk about them!

Let this example of a physical injury also help illustrate the way I minimize my mental grievances to those around me. Even the words "ankle" and "sprain" put in conjunction makes my eyes roll. It is such a dumb injury, in my opinion. I feel like shoulder injuries are badass, extremely painful, and annoying, but cooler than an ankle sprain. You get a shoulder injury from playing a contact sport like football. Literally the only way you sprain your ankle is by falling. I fall a lot. Ugh, so lame.

I had my first asinine fall that ripped the ligaments surrounding my foot when I was thirteen years old. I was at a dance team practice and landed improperly out of a jump. My ankle turned as my foot made contact with the ground and next thing I knew, I was lying down on our school's brand-new turf field, unable to stand up. I recall a popping sound and my eyes were sealed with pain so all I could see was darkness. It fucking sucked. I went in to see my doctor and he put me on crutches and into a large black, obnoxious boot that went up to my knee. I guess it was pretty severe; the swelling was unlike anything I had seen before. No exaggeration, it looked like a baseball had welcomed itself in its new home, my outer ankle. I could not apply weight on it for a long time.

The injury at dance occurred a week or two before I was scheduled to begin high school, so yeah, I had to crutch around the hallways of a brand-new building. I had no idea where any of my classes were, and OMG, there were so many cute older boys! What a nightmare. I tried my best to distract from the giant boot and crutches with a cute dress and some killer side bangs. Mind you, I also had braces at the time, so I was certainly a sight for sore eyes. It is still a wonder how I managed to make any friends. I remember still trying my darndest to look cute by wearing a neon green, blue and white checkered dress. I hobbled around the halls, lost amidst the crowd of new faces, searching for my classes. I still am baffled at how in the world the tall sophomore boy on the lacrosse team I had a crush on did not instantly love me back!

I do not remember having any other bad ankle sprains in high school, although I am sure there were one or two more that are blending together in my memory. I recall a few in college. Luckily, I had a good physical therapist in Buffalo who was able to tend to my aching body. Since that initial injury when I was thirteen years old, it has become a tale as old as time. A jump in rehearsal, an improper landing, a pop, black, tears, ice, sitting on my couch embarrassed, hating life for a couple weeks. I have also had numerous ankle rolls doing silly everyday tasks, like walking down the fucking street. Yeah. I shit you not; I have rolled an ankle while putting coins into a parking meter. Face palm. Least badass injury possible.

Yesterday, I was on a nice happiness kick. I had been going through a depressive couple of weeks and finally arrived on the other side, thanks to some great dance classes, my friends, and you know, making myself laugh by putting my dumb tweets on ironic, inspirational photos in the Word Swag app. The stupidity of it all still makes me giggle. I even have a new crush! This shit makes me feel *alive,* man, even if I know it is not realistic. I was happily trotting from my car to dance class. I had been writing all day and was really looking forward to the two classes I had booked for the night. I had friends meeting me there and I rearranged my work schedule so that I could take these couple classes.

I was a little late for class and walking quickly along the shitty LA sidewalk in my sneakers. I was staring down at my phone, giggling at my own Instagram story for the hundredth time. There was a considerable dip in the sidewalk where the large concrete tile ended, and a patch of brick began. It was too much for my poor right ankle to take and down I went. My steel water bottle rolled down the street, making a loud clang. I fell to my hands and knees. Luckily, I have become such a professional at falling that I can always catch myself so I never hit my face on the ground. No, I prefer to get my concussions from walking into walls in the middle of the night. Yep, true story. It was dark.

Anyway, this particular fall was hard and totally painful. There was a man walking towards me on the sidewalk. He was tan, wearing khaki shorts, losing his hair, and likely in his late fifties. His initial reaction to my fall was something totally normal like, "Oh gosh! Are you okay?!" I imagine what a sane person would do in my situation—maybe take a deep breath, thank the man for his concern, and welcome his outstretched assistance-offering hand? Nope, not me! I laughed while saying "OW" and/or a curse word, but I quickly distorted my natural in-pain face to something more pleasant to protect this random *stranger* from any upset. I then assured him that I was great. HUH?! Because I told him I was okay, he quickly laughed and made a cheap middle-aged joke, "It's because you were on your phone, isn't it?!"

I stood up slowly, picked up all of my belongings that had fallen, and decided that I was not happy with his reaction, even though it was probably inspired by my own lightheartedness. I furrowed my brow and said, "Maybe, but also the sidewalk is uneven as fuck, dude."

He egged on, "JUST ADMIT IT, YOU WERE ON YOUR PHONE, HA HA!" Old people get so hard off tearing us millennials apart; I could write an entire separate book on how mad this makes me. Ya know what, sir? The stupid shit I do on my phone actually inspired me to write this book, so how is *that* for ya?! His persistence was annoying, so with some frustration, but also still humor in my voice, I went for "Way to kick me while I am down, dude, jeez!" and limped away.

I am satisfied with that reaction. He did not deserve for me to be rude as hell, but also, come on, guys, this man sucks and probably spends his Friday nights eating TV dinners, regretting how much money his divorce cost him. Pardon me. Clearly I am still a little salty about all of that.

I have been thinking a lot about that event, probably because it happened last night, but also because of how the rest of the evening played out. I was pissed off about the way the man had reacted to my fall, but I realized I was partly to blame for sugarcoating the severity of my injury. I was in a tremendous amount of pain, but he had no way of knowing that. He was unaware of the fact that I had just recovered from a previous sprain mere months ago and was finally dancing the way I wanted to again. He did not even know I was a dancer. He did not know I had been looking forward to, living even, for tonight's dance classes to which I was en route. He did not know that dance was one of the only things I could rely on for happiness. He did not know that I lose my mind without dance when I am forced to rest due to an injury.

I probably should have turned around, walked back to my car, and driven straight home to some ice and elevation, but I could not bring myself to do the responsible thing. I hobbled down the road in a huff, assuming it was probably one of my minor rolls that would heal itself in a couple days. I remember having some self-awareness in that moment. I shook my head at myself limping to a dance class. *Girl, you are crazy*, I thought. I pondered over the chapter I had just written about balance and cringed at myself for willingly disobeying my own advice. I could not bring myself to go home.

To be fair, I did not realize the severity of the injury, and in that moment, I needed dance. I pushed through two tricky dance classes; that is three hours of dancing. I was in pain the whole time. "Why?" you ask. Because dance is why I live. I was meeting my friends there and I may or may not have been hoping to see a cute guy I know in class. Yup, I had officially lost it. It was one of the most physically self-harming things I have ever done. I still, the next morning, could not bring myself to fully regret it. I know for a fact that I made the injury worse by dancing on it right away and I sure did pay the price.

I told my friends in class what happened, and they begged the question, "Wait, are you seriously okay?"

I assured them that I was. "Yup, it happens all the time. I'll just ice when I get home!" Don't worry about me! Why? Because my ankle sprains are embarrassing and frequent, so I pretend to be fine. The purpose of this chapter is not to ponder on my ankle sprains but to explore why the hell I am always protecting others from my pain by pretending to be okay when I am seriously not.

The Dance of Self-blame, Yay

One of my favorite realizations I made into a joke (obviously) when I tweeted a meme paired with something like, *this is me questioning whether my tendency to blame myself for everything is low self-worth or narcissism.* I think it is both. I love this joke because for the longest time, my ego convinced me that I took everything so personally because I was hurting on the inside. I am not sure what exactly caused me to check my big fat head and make this realization before I sent out that tweet, but I do remember laughing for days about it.

Some things are your fault—that is okay. We are all human. Just take responsibility and move forward. Be an adult, obviously; do not be a piece of shit. But isn't it slightly arrogant of you to infer that it is your fault that it rained, ruining your friend's party that you helped plan? Who do you think you are, God? I was in a therapy session recently, trying to figure out why my initial reaction to negative situations involving other people is to take the blame. My therapist and I were discussing an instance when a guy had done me wrong. Shocker, right? It turned out to be entirely his fault; he was acting borderline insane, but of course, I thought *I* was the crazy one for a minute before I checked myself, thank God.

"Why do I always feel like it's my fault when something does not go the way I want it to?" I asked my therapist.

"You take responsibility for other people's behaviors and feelings because what happens when you are responsible for something?" she egged me on.

"I CAN CONTROL IT!" I nearly leapt off her comfy couch and into her fern. Aha! I am going to repeat this to you guys because it is so crucial. I, and probably some of you, blame myself and embody guilt and fault for other's behaviors, actions, and feelings because if I was responsible for those things, I would be able to change them. But I am not, so I can't. I know, I want everyday life to pan out perfectly, the way I dream it up in my head at night, but that just is not the way it goes, is it? We cannot control time, the weather, or the people around us. Therefore, we cannot take responsibility for them. Surrender. Worry about ya damn self.

Additionally, I realized my responsibility logic was working in reverse for me. When I had achieved great accomplishments, people would congratulate me only for me to brush it off. "Awww. Well, I had a lot of help." Does this sound familiar to you? I see a lot of people doing this. We diminish and minimize our own victories all of the goddamn time. I have decided that this is self-abuse and I am currently working tirelessly to fix it. You should too, boo!

As tempted as I am to spend all day writing thank yous into the acknowledgment section of this book, deep down I know that no one wrote it but me. My creative-as-hell ideas were born in my own mind, so here we are. I was the one who spent months editing instead of watching Netflix, no one else. There ya have it! No more minimizing our achievements, guys. Be grateful to those around you but also be grateful to your damn self. And do not be afraid to ask for help when you need it! Group tattoo date to get these vows inked all over our forearms? My treat!

Ya Know What? I Am Not Okay.

When I begin to grow weary over some trouble I find in my life, my mind likes to tell me I should not fret. *Oh, you're upset your crush got back together with his girlfriend? Don't worry, girl, it's not personal; they're bonded by years of oxytocin.* These thought patterns can be somewhat healthy but not when you begin to completely stuff down your feelings with them. Silencing natural emotions is no good either, my good people. Hell no, the actions of any man are not personal to me, but that does not change the fact that the guy toyed with me and then ultimately chose someone else. That hurts, and that is okay. *Oh yeah, my eating disorder is a thing, but I am okay, hehe.* Fuck that. Most days I am in so much motherfucking pain, you guys. *Yeah, I loved that guy a lot, but the distance made it impossible for us to be together, but I will be okay!* Actually, life without him feels like there is a giant gaping hole in my chest. *It is just a migraine. I get them all of the time, no problem. I can do the dance sixteen more times!* FUCKING OW! I can't see, bitch!

When thoughts of pain or disturbance arise, I dilute them with reasons I should not be feeling said pain. Kinda fucked up, right? Sure, we are hashtag blessed to have the problems we do and the time to worry about our grievances, but that does not mean we should ignore them. You guys know how much of a feeler I am so you will be shocked to hear me when I tell you I recently had a midday mental breakdown and cried rigorously for the first time in three months. I was triggered by an emotional conversation with my mother over this book (ha ha) and everything came bubbling to the surface. The pain from the breakup I was suppressing with my eating disorder poured out of my eyes like torrential rain.

A few months prior to this episode, I was sexually assaulted. The pain from that event (which I will go into more detail later on), was a lot to handle so I stuffed it down with obsessive, restrictive dieting habits. On this day, all of the pain from having my body taken advantage of, which I had been ignoring, erupted. So did the pain from my eating disorder, which I had been numbing by obsessing over men. The pain from those impossible men's rejection of me that I suppressed with social media, television, weed, and sleep was there too. It was all there, eagerly waiting to be felt. My dog licked the tears off my face as I christened my new apartment with my first mental breakdown. The sheer shock of my realization that this was the first instance in which I cried, or felt any emotion for that matter, in the apartment I had been living in for months, hit me like a tsunami wave.

The moral of all of this—do not suppress pain, or any emotion, especially for the benefit of someone else's feelings.

It will come out in its own time, so do not try to force it either. When she comes, and she comes a-blazing, sit with her. Feel that shit. It is completely and utterly healing, and yes, you have to disregard the fact that your neighbors might be able to hear your concerning wailing.

Sometimes, I allow myself to get super angsty and whine about how *no one understands me, wahh!* But I am learning more and more that the walls I put up play a big role in this. I feel like an outsider a lot of the time, like the things I say and feel do not make sense to other people. It could be because I am a special snowflake artist with a weird sense of humor who enjoys her alone time a little too much, but it also could be because I expect people to see me without me having to do the work of showing them who I am. People can't read our minds; we have to tell them what is going on inside us. It is okay to be in pain. You can tell your friends that you are not okay for once. We will all survive. Your life depends on it, actually.

Chapter Ten

Healthy Fats
All Damn Day Son

Anxiety

It is safe to conclude that a ton of people my age have struggled with some form of an anxiety disorder at one point or another. Yeah, sure, go ahead, point your fingers at us and our iPhone use. I am sure advancement of technology, over-access to information, and the speed at which our world moves these days is partly to blame.

I moved to Los Angeles in February of 2017. My anxiety disorder began to manifest in October of that same year. I did a lot of research about mental health conditions in order to better understand my own, so I am not just pulling this out of my ass, I promise. Those who are at risk for generalized anxiety disorder are typically what psychologists refer to as "biologically sensitive." This means we are acutely sensitive to external *and* internal stimuli. In my case, I can experience biological sensitivity in the form of extreme, fervid empathy. Not to sound too LA zen hippie-dippie, but I can feel the energies of the people around me and I almost always react and adapt to them. If someone across the room becomes disturbed, so do I.

External sensitivity can also be as simple as noticing subtle changes to your environment, like when a different car that is not usually there is parked in the lot of your apartment complex. Internal biological sensitivity may include the ability to pinpoint the origin of physical discomfort in the body to a tee or knowing you are on the verge of a migraine. I had to confront the reality that I am not in fact psychic, just really in tune with my body. Darn.

The second factor that puts you at risk for anxiety is a slew of lovely personality traits that many of us have. These include crippling perfectionism, worrying too much, seeking to please others, and holding ourselves, and those around us, to unrealistically high standards. Um, is this my Tinder bio? When I read these risk factors in a book about anxiety, I felt hauntingly understood. According to researchers (a.k.a. people who are way smarter than me), if you have these qualities, you are a ticking anxiety disorder time bomb waiting to happen. Sorry!

The third element that causes anxiety disorders is a sudden onset and overload of stress. This is what sets off that sweet time bomb. Being alone in Los Angeles, away from everyone I knew, and pursuing an incredibly stressful career undoubtedly contributed to the onset of stress that triggered my anxiety disorder. My days were filled with grunt work and tension. I was driving through the country's worst traffic to unfamiliar locations, attending intimidating classes and auditions, desperately trying to get myself settled into some sort of rhythm. Even grocery stores stressed me out!

I remember my first time in a Ralph's a day or two after I moved. It was time to start anew and purchase those items that you usually only have to buy once every five years: baking soda, vanilla extract, and a huge bag of lentils that I have probably only touched once since. The inside corners of my eyes welled up with tears, causing my vision to blur as I shuffled along that sticky, shiny floor. I wandered down the same aisles with my squeaky cart over and over again, unable to locate the peanut butter. You know how when you have been going to the same grocery store for a long time you can mindlessly accomplish your chore without a bead of sweat? To make first-world problem matters worse, the grocery store I was used to back home is actually the highest ranked in the United States and they do not have it in California. Hi, Wegmans, Mama misses you! So yeah, there I was, lost in Ralph's, wondering if *this* was the factor of my relocation that was going to break me. Not leaving my family, not being in a new state alone, or the long-distance relationship I was trying to make work. Nope, the grocery store was going to be the change that would be too much to handle.

Fast-forward a few months into the southwestern heat of the biggest life change I had gone through thus far. I became the worst version of myself for a little while. I had reached what some like to call a breaking point. So here I am going to tell you yet another unsexy story about myself, and yes it also involves my ex, Tyler. Get ready to add this to the list of embarrassing stories included in this book. As I have mentioned before, this relationship, my most recent, was mostly healthy, so please go easy on me—this was probably the lowest point in my relationship with him.

Forgive me. A lot of time has passed, and I have done a considerable amount of maturing and spent hundreds of hours on the couch of a mental health professional since this cringeworthy incident occurred. I can assure you that I do *not* act or think like this anymore. This event is not what caused my anxiety disorder, but it definitely kick-started it into motion. I am currently cringing right now at the thought, wincing at my naiveté.

A few months after my big transfer to LA, while we were still together, Tyler traveled with two of his guy friends to Greece for his well-deserved post-bar exam vacation. I truly wanted him to have a great time and knew that no one had earned that trip more than he did after studying sun up to sundown for months on end. He traveled with a tour company that organizes trips for young travelers. I actually assisted him with the booking process because I had done a similar trip to Italy and Greece when I was twenty and single. Thinking back on how I thotted it up on that trip was definitely triggering for me and I spent most of the nights he was out and about with his single-guy friends worrying like crazy. I trusted this man; he was always so wonderful to me and I knew he would never cheat. Unfortunately, this was not enough to prevent my traumatic past experiences with unfaithful men from haunting my mind while he was having the time of his life on this trip.

I was glued to my phone, anxiously awaiting his text message updates, replaying his Snapchats, and stalking his Instagram to see if he had started following any new hot girls (this is a miserable way to live, guys. I look back with such regret). I guess I can be gracious with myself and remember that I was engaging in these self-destructive habits due to past trauma. Blame my first love, remember him?! You know I am kidding. I am an adult and now take responsibility for these habits and do my very best to no longer take myself down these damaging paths. I knew Tyler would not cheat on me. What I feared was that he would want to. That there would be someone so gorgeous on this trip who he fancied and that he would resent *me* for being the girlfriend that prevented him from acting on said desire. My mind is fun, isn't it?

So, the trip drew to a close and he headed to California almost immediately to see me. There had been no news of infidelity and it seemed to have been a wonderful time (but not too wonderful without me, if you know what I mean, right, ladies?). Still, a twinge of insecurity would stab my gut when he would talk about the girl his roommate slept with, the night they stayed up until the sun came up, or the sick club they went to. I found myself engaging in manipulation tactics out of my own insecurities, like not acting happy for him or being a bore talking about how much I hate nightclubs. Again, my bad. Yikes, I am so sorry, Tyler. World, I promise you, I was doing this obliviously, and I am proud to say I have learned my lesson due to all this soul searching. I am a catch now, I swear!

A few months later, on a different visit when we were vacationing in Florida, my insecurities were robbing me of my peace of mind, as they so often did in relationships, so I brought it up to him while we were out together at a bar. Naturally, he was frustrated with me because this was not the first time I had sought validation from him. Our conversation resulted in him informing me of a situation that occurred when he was in Greece. A girl in his tour group followed him back to his hotel one night and asked if he wanted to hook up. He is a loyal man and I believed him when he told me he declined politely and then explained that he had a girlfriend and showed her photos of me.

I trusted him when he told me all of this, but my heart began to speed up as if I was driving seventy-five miles an hour on the freeway and suddenly lost control of the vehicle. My body went into full-on fight-or-flight mode. I wondered what she looked like, what her name was, what she did for a living, was she skinnier than me? I begged these questions to Tyler through sobs, in a fit of rage and hysteria. As if knowing any of these factors would give me any control over the situation that had already passed.

I am not sure that telling his over-jealous girlfriend this story was the best idea on Tyler's part, given that nothing came of it except my headfirst dive further into insanity. I do know it came from a place of love and his desire to express to me how deeply I should trust his devotion to me. But I lost any grip I had on reality. To me, this is what anxiety is—a loss of the present day and the present moment and instead becoming transfixed and obsessed with fearful thoughts.

My days became consumed with an idea of this woman. Had he *wanted* to sleep with her, even though he didn't? Would he resent me for preventing this romantic lay in an exciting, sexy country? I could feel that I had no control over what Tyler was thinking. As previously noted, my life at the time was all over the place with the move and everything. It is embarrassing to me that a fit of insecure jealously would trigger my anxiety disorder. What happened was this: I had this awful idea and fear of what would happen on Tyler's trip. I fantasized about all of the reasons he might wish he was not dating me. The night I found out that one of my fears came so close to fruition, my craziness was validated, sort of.

Now I am comfortable settling on the idea that fuck yeah, I am sure he would have slept with her had he been single 'cause he is a guy and that is what guys do best. I like to imagine that if a situation like this came up in a future relationship, I would be way cool about it. Hell, maybe I'd even let him go through with the hookup as long as boundaries were set. She is cute, she has an accent, you will never see her again, why not? I have never been in an open relationship before, but I am infinitely curious as to how I would handle some type of leniency now that I am at peace with the laws of attraction. Maybe I will report back to you guys in the book I write in my thirties. Stay tuned!

Circling back to my outbreak of anxiety. After that trip to Florida ended, we each went back to our respective homes. I started going crazy in LA. I couldn't focus on my everyday tasks. I had no local friends to keep me out of my head. What I did have was work and dance, and thank heavens I did. Minor disturbances would set me off during this time. I would jump at loud noises, awake with a racing heart, unable to fall asleep at night, and take myself into mindless internet-stalking episodes that led me to frantically call Tyler in the middle of the night, desperate for consolation and reassurance.

I have always loved coffee, but now that I had general anxiety, I began to find that panic attacks would come in the mornings shortly following my caffeine spike. Lowering my intake and switching to tea helped this, but I felt heartbroken, reminiscing on the calm weekend days in college where I would mosey around my Buffalo apartment on Saturdays, drinking an entire pot of coffee throughout the day as I cleaned and studied in my fuzzy bathrobe. Those days were gone. Here I was in LA, having episodes that felt like heart attacks.

I remember having to excuse myself to the bathroom at work to break down and cry. I would shake with fear. Fear of what exactly, I did not know. I began to check out books on anxiety from the library because I was determined to better understand what was happening.

At this time, I was also jumping around to different therapists; I had not yet settled on one I was comfortable committing to. Eventually, I found one on my insurance website who specialized in anxiety, depression, and eating disorders. She seemed perfect for me. She was my fourth LA therapist and I still see her today. If you find yourself discouraged after meeting one or two therapists, I urge you to shop around. Not everyone is for you and not every health professional is great at their job, even if they do have that degree! Be picky and find one who you feel comfortable with and who helps and sees you.

Cognitive behavioral therapy (CBT) really helped me understand my triggers, my thought patterns, and how to challenge them. Anxiety stems from fear. Mine comes from fear of the unknown, fear of failure, fear of heartbreak, and fear of disappointing others and myself. I learned how to replace these haunting "what-ifs" that my mind would draw up with rational thinking. Therapy, caffeine reduction, weight lifting, spending time with friends, and meditation helped me begin to feel like myself again. The brain is like a muscle and all of these practices need to be worked routinely.

Thankfully, I am so much better now. I have not had a panic attack in quite some time. I feel pride in the fact that I have mostly beaten the thing even though I still have to work diligently at it. In order to stay calm in my daily life, I continue these practices and I encourage you to do the same if you are struggling with this shitty, shitty feeling. *10% Happier* by Dan Harris is a great read I recommend for anyone with anxiety. Or even for those of you simply interested in mindfulness, which you should be, ya bum. It will turn even the largest of skeptics into meditation advocates.

Mental health problems are not a weakness, my dudes. Please do not forget that. I spent a lot of time worrying that my anxiety made me a bad employee, friend, daughter, girlfriend, and whatnot. Trust me, these thoughts have crossed my mind a million times—*my mind will prevent me from being successful; my anxiety makes me hard to love; my anxiety makes me a fragile, pathetic human.* These were all worries I toyed with inside my head until one day, a guy I dated said he did not want to commit to me because my mental health struggles could pose a problem in the future. There are so many reasons I could argue with this (we all have our demons. At least I am aware of mine and actively work on them). But in that particular moment, I realized all of the ways my battle with anxiety had in fact made me a better person. It took someone telling me my anxiety was a weakness to realize it was a strength.

I came to my own defense when he said that and I realized that deep down, I did not even believe all the insulting lies I was telling myself! Anxiety disorders form for countless different reasons—caring a little too much, perfectionism, being a risk taker, and so on. These are all qualities I actually adore about myself and would not take back in a million years. Why should I be punished for them? I developed an anxiety disorder as a result of the building blocks that make me who I am. I would not change any of those qualities, no matter how hard it gets sometimes. They make me, me. I am who I am today because of my anxiety. I am more self-aware thanks to my anxiety. I am stronger than ever thanks to my anxiety. I am a more sensitive, empathetic person because of my anxiety. I know how it feels to walk into a room only to have it spin and instantly begin to sweat with paranoia, so I can be a better friend to others who may be experiencing that sensation. I am a more well-equipped friend, lover, professional, and overall human being because of my anxiety. I have no shame, and neither should you.

Depression

I do not believe I have the devastating condition that is clinical depression but there have been a handful of dark days of my life when I have felt the lowest of low, unsure it would ever end. I want to share those days with you in case you can relate.

My overthinking is usually what causes me to feel depressed. It has led me down some pretty dark paths. I take my dog for long walks every morning that I can. I love to entertain myself on these walks with music albums, audiobooks, and podcasts. One morning, when the time had arrived for a walk, I was already in a hole of overthinking. My mind had been racing out of control ever since I had heard some troubling news regarding Adrenaline Guy the night before. I was coming off twelve hours straight of hurriedly imagining conversations with him to confront the situation. I had also been dealing with some body-image issues for the past couple weeks. Considering all the madness that my mind was mulling over, I was looking forward to walking it out with my girl. My current audiobook was extremely interesting, and I was looking forward to spending some time with it this morning.

Approximately fifteen minutes into my walk, I realized that my mind was still a racing frenzy, spinning out of control, and I had not heard a single word of what the narrator of the book was reading to me. The text was playing directly into my ears, but it was not entering my brain because it was too preoccupied. I frantically rewound my book and promised myself I would focus this time. I ended up walking Pinot for about an hour that morning and pretty much the entire walk consisted of this dance: mentally drifting away, coming back to earth, frantically rewinding the audio, only to drift away again.

In the spring morning glow, I was taken inside the western-style homes of southern California that we were walking by. My imagination brought me past the cacti in the front yards, through the windows, and into their kitchens. I wondered if all of those people enjoyed their little worlds; a desperate attempt to escape from my own. The smell of freshly mowed grass had always brought on a sense of nostalgia, but that morning, it was enough to bring me to tears as it reminded me of New York summers, my family, and lost love. All of these beautiful, sad realities played themselves out to me as my Audible book attempted to teach me about childhood trauma. I heard none of it.

My extremely low mood that day prompted me to sit down and write. For me, healing from these tough days is a matter of taking care of myself, possibly by writing, meditating, calling a friend, and simply riding the wave. These tough feelings come in waves but fortunately for me, every time they come, they eventually pass.

This experience also reminds me of a day that should have been a great day, but turned out to be pretty terrible—I have my brain chemicals to thank for that. A couple years ago, I was vacationing in Prague with some of my best friends. At that time in my life, I had just graduated college and was packing up for my big move to Los Angeles. It was a scary time, preceding what would be one of the hardest years of my life. I was undoubtedly aware of that. We were well into our European trip and had been enjoying ourselves with carbs and alcohol and no end in sight. I recall sitting down for breakfast one morning and eating some delicious food in a huge, elegant restaurant with tablecloths and large windows. I was feeling pretty rough that morning, which I blamed on fatigue, hunger, and a hangover. But after we finished eating and I consumed enough coffee to kill a small child, a darkness washed over me.

I recall watching this couple that was sitting to my left. It was a beautiful Czech woman eating breakfast with an older man. She sat with her back arched, had tight jeans on, bore a gorgeous body, and had long black hair that swam down to her waist. Her elbows were propped up on the table and I decided that the older man loved her. I began to think about love and all of my insecurities. I now realize that I fantasize a lot about the lives of others when I am sad. My eyes felt heavy, there was a weight in my chest, and I was sitting at the table with my friends, but I was not really there. Their jokes and the conversation were going over my head.

I excused myself to the fancy restroom that was atop a marble staircase. When I got to a stall, I broke down. Sobs erupted. I felt so unexplainably sad. The world around me did not feel right and it had nothing to do with the fact that I was in a foreign country. I must have been in there a while and Lindsey must have picked up on my mood at the table because eventually she joined me in the bathroom.

Lindsey has been one of my closest friends since the seventh grade and she has a lovely ability to bring calm to the most stressful of situations and light to even the darkest of days. Anyone who knows her knows that she not only looks like a Victoria's Secret Angel, but she has the persona of an angel as well. Her sweet voice, logic, and hugs were exactly what I needed in that moment. She knew I was not feeling well and I had a hard time explaining why because nothing was noticeably wrong. Nothing bad had happened and we had been having the time of our lives up until this point. This cloud looming over me felt both internal and external. It felt chemical and intrinsic. I suspected all of the alcohol we were consuming at dinner and the late nights had caught up to me.

I have noticed a pattern in recent years that when I drink heavily, my hangovers tend to include a very low, often depressive mood. At the time, I was also on an antidepressant I had been taking for a few years to treat my chronic migraines. My migraines had gotten worse, so a few weeks before our trip, my doctor increased my dose. It is strange because the medication is supposed to combat depression and a number of other issues, not cause it. Still, I was no longer willing to take any chances because the state I was in that day felt harrowingly dangerous. I decided to never take another one of those pills again. You, my friend, should consult your doctor before making any changes to your medications. Remember, do as I say, not as I do.

The day progressed and we decided to catch a train out to the catacombs that were way outside of the city. Interestingly, I was about to engage in one of the darkest tourist activities on one of the darkest days of my life. It was a cold winter day and I copped a window seat in a box on the train with my friends. It was quiet, the boys napping, Lindsey listening to something in her headphones. I pulled out my journal to catch up on documenting the trip (something I do every time I travel) and spent a lot of time looking out the window. It was a dreary, gray countryside, barren by cold and winter. We passed average-looking houses of white and brown and fields covered in snow.

Despite being a writer, I still cannot fully describe the way I felt that day. Actually, I remember looking through the glass, feeling fascinated by the feeling. *So, this is what depression is. Damn.* I felt like I could understand human beings a lot more in that moment. This is a morbid thought, but I keep it real with you because you guys are my best buds—that day, I understood suicide. I felt so terrible and depressed that *yup, if I felt like this all the time, I would want out too.* I wondered if this feeling was there to stay, but part of me was hopeful it would go away.

I am still not sure exactly when or how the cloud disappeared, but somewhere among the bones of the brave Czech dead, it did. I am so thankful I was around friends that day, and again, I am not a psychologist, and I do not understand the scientific logistics of how or why this episode occurred. Staying away from antidepressants and migraine medication has helped me and I gather that my constant therapy also keeps dark feelings at bay. Depression is a scary thing. If you are struggling or have ever struggled with it, I urge you to seek professional help. Please also know that I love you dearly and wish for you to feel relief from that terrible feeling I only got a minor taste of that day.

There was another day recently that felt full of darkness and despair and I was having a difficult time pulling myself out of it. Blame Mercury or blame me, but I *had* to do something to feel better. After a morning of work, I decided to drive to the coast and sit by the water. I call this a "depression drive." I am lucky to live in a part of the world that allows me to breathe in the salty Pacific and witness her rhythm whenever I have a free couple of hours. Something about driving along the Pacific Coast Highway and listening to music grounds me and reminds me that life is in fact worth living.

If you are not as hashtag blessed as I am to live in or around Los Angeles (do not worry, we are probably going to break off soon during an earthquake) I urge you to find your own place to take yourself on a depression drive, or walk. Find somewhere nice to sit by yourself for a couple hours and tune into your thoughts. Most of the time, if you sit there long enough, they will begin to tell you what's up.

This recent depression drive of mine was surrounded by feelings of loneliness, emptiness, frustration, and helplessness. I did not know exactly what I went to the beach for, but I certainly found it. I watched surfers paddle rapidly, coasting smoothly along the top of huge waves and crashing down repeatedly. I watched couples cuddle romantically next to one another on towels. I watched girls in bikinis dance to a Spanish song. I watched as a young boy, possibly eight or nine, held his baby sister in his arms and walked with her in the wake as their mother followed close behind. The boy was facing the ocean as he gave the baby a kiss on her cheek. He then turned his face to her and the baby, no older than one, pecked him back with a proud smooch right on the lips. It was one of the cutest fuckin' things I have ever seen in my life.

Love was the word that whispered through my mind that instant, lingering like a puff of smoke. *Love. That is the reason to live.* Then, after watching that beautiful family make its way down the beach, I made a list in my phone of the reasons I wanted to keep living.

The Pacific Ocean
Saltwater air
To kiss again
To be kissed again
Because I have not drunk all the wine
Because I need to rescue more dogs in my life
To laugh
To publish this book
To bring what only I can into the world of dance
To inspire
To feel emotions and to cry more tears
To see my friends again
To see my brother get married
To bring a child of my own into the world
To attend another outdoor concert in the summer
To create more blissful memories
To travel further
To hear a new song
To hear a song I have heard a million times
To fall in love again

Some of the concepts on my list may seem minute; some seem momentous. Make one for yourself, please. Love you.

Acne

Just when you thought things couldn't get sexier here, behold the most glamorous content yet! Fellas, buckle up because your dream girl is about to get into her best feature—acne, yay! As I type this, I am coming at you live with scabs all over my arms and back due to a reaction from a harsh skin treatment I just did in a desperate attempt to clear it. In the past when I have preached on social media about my skin struggles, my followers have been baffled and sent me messages like "WTF? you have perfect skin!" GIRL, have you heard of a filter? My social media accounts pose as an advertisement for my skill set, so featuring my acne is definitely not something I do.

For those of you who are skeptical about the severity of the skin issues I have had to deal with, I have attached some photos later in this chapter. For the millions of you who have a crush on me, I guarantee these pictures will make that go away. You're welcome!

I was pretty lucky in adolescence when it came to acne. In the genre of shaping my eyebrows and not blushing around cute boys, not so much. I had a few breakouts here and there but nothing that was ever bad enough to land me in a doctor's office. I always had pretty good skin until three months into living in Los Angeles, when the entire bottom half of my face erupted in pimples. It was painful and embarrassing. I stopped taking photos of myself and began seeing pricey aestheticians and dermatologists. The first dermatologist I found was old, male, and white. He would see me in his room for about three minutes per appointment. He'd then quickly shoo me out of the office with another prescription for antibiotics month after month.

To be fair, the antibiotics cleared my face over time, but we all know that they are not a permanent solution. I would ask him if maybe we could begin to wean off them or why my hands broke out in painful rashes when I was outside. He would dismiss my concerns by telling me to wear sunscreen, keep taking the pills, and *I'll see you in a month*. Eventually, I stopped seeing this negligent man and took matters into my own sunburned hands by slowly lowering my dosage and opting for topical treatments like facials and chemical peels.

About a month or two into experiencing anxiety for the first time in my life, now six months into living in LA, my left arm broke out in a rash of tiny red bumps beginning at the top of my shoulder and extending down to a few inches above my elbow. Some of the bumps were tiny with whiteheads; others were large and tender. This lovely spread made my arm itch constantly. I was mortified. I covered it up with clothing and became absolutely disgusted with myself. I made an appointment with a new dermatologist after a couple months of Google and tea tree oil were not seeming to solve the problem. At my first visit, my new dermatologist suspected that it was keratosis pilaris (KP), a skin condition that causes red bumps by blocking the hair follicles. The treatment plan we tried following that appointment did not help at all. If anything, my condition worsened over the course of a few more months and now *both* of my arms were covered in bumps.

I cannot even begin to describe how mortified I felt. If you have had acne in your life, you know what I am talking about. I felt helpless and out of control. I was embarrassed to show skin, to be around friends or strangers, or even to be intimate with sexual partners. After we ruled out KP, the doctor took some samples of the skin to test them in the lab to see if it was some sort of fungal or bacterial infection. I remember those long weeks when I was awaiting the test results. It was now springtime of that following year and I could not ever envision myself having clear skin again. I pictured myself on the beach that summer with disgusting pimples. I feared the warm weather because that would make my skin more difficult to cover. I was so self-conscious.

This dermatologist gave me a topical steroid to use in the interim. This also made the condition worse. At this point both of my arms and chest were now covered in red pustules. Desperately awaiting the lab results or any type of solution, I was constantly googling and crying myself to sleep. I felt as though I had lost a part of myself.

I scheduled an appointment with an allergist to get a test. I had been under the care of this new dermatologist for months and there was still no sign of a solution. I remember that allergist visit vividly. A kind young nurse took me back and asked a bunch of questions about my symptoms as she took down notes. Eventually the allergist came in to have a look. I timidly removed my outer layer to reveal the hundreds of blemishes that covered my body and stole my self-confidence. He scanned my exposed body with eyes of concern. He pulled up his wheelie stool and sat down in front of me and told me that he could tell just by looking and hearing about my experience that "it was a dermatological issue, not an allergy." Luckily, that saved me the agony of having to go through with an allergy test.

I was exhausted. I had been poked and prodded for months and the light at the end of the tunnel was nowhere in sight. To his misfortune, I began to weep into this allergist's arms. He handled my breakdown impeccably and he made me feel understood. I felt superficial and embarrassed to be crying over something so vain that seemed to just be an aesthetic flaw. Factually, I knew I was so lucky to not be facing a tragic, life-threatening medical condition, but that did not take away from the fact that I felt as though my identity had been stripped away. I told him I had been to multiple dermatologists but had seen no improvement despite the countless number of treatments. He urged me to keep trying and to get another opinion. He soothed me by insisting that "there is a solution somewhere out there."

After I calmed down, he sent me upstairs to the office of a dermatologist he recommended. I left his office after checking out and walked straight to the new dermatologist with his referral in hand. I still had tears in my eyes as I gave the kind receptionists my name and requested an appointment. They must have known I was on the brink of a psychotic break or Jesus came down to earth because they fit me in with one of their physician assistants right then and there.

My time in that room in the back of the office was a blur. They had to have brought in a total of five or six professionals throughout the visit, starting with the physician assistant and a couple nursing aids. My main physician was pretty sure it was just a plague of acne, but she called in the main doctor to be sure. He was rigid with me and asked me what supplements I was taking. I told him birth control pills, the occasional multivitamin, and a scoop of protein powder. He asked me about steroid use. I told him about the topical steroid the previous dermatologist gave me, and he informed me that was definitely making it worse. He seemed convinced I was taking oral steroids which was A) flattering because I did not realize my arms were that jacked and B) slightly insulting for ethical reasons, of course.

This man was so confident in the fact that I was taking oral steroids that I honestly questioned myself. He had a medical degree and a fancy white coat, which were so intimidating to me, I kid you not, I thought about it again. Maybe he was right. *Was* I taking steroids? Clearly, my low self-confidence and unwavering trust in authority had gotten to me. I insisted I was not, incredibly worried all the people in scrubs surrounding me would assume I was lying.

He formulated a plan of action in which I stop taking "EVERYTHING" I was taking. And I was to pick up this new strain of antibiotics, use a benzoyl-peroxide bodywash they provided me, and begin using a clindamycin phosphate cream on the affected area every day. I was in. Their certainty that the issue was acne, which could be caused by many factors, including my steroid use (HA), hormonal changes, stress, gluten, dairy, the polluted air and water of LA, and so on gave me hope that they could also provide a solution once and for all.

The doctor exited swiftly, and the aids gathered my prescriptions. As all this was going on, the physician assistant told me she was going to go through and do some extractions. I have had many facials, so this was nothing new to me. It's something I find quite satisfying, actually. Turns out, extractions in a dermatologist office are a different experience than they are at a spa. She used metal tools that looked like razor blades and started to go at my skin aggressively. The fluorescent overhead lights were blinding and as I was sitting in that plastic chair, I started to lose feeling in my legs. She was quickly moving around the affected areas and I began to bleed. It had been such an overwhelming afternoon, filled with a lot of emotion, so the sight of blood dripping from my chest and arms was just enough to put me over the edge. I lost vision in both of my eyes and the nausea was undeniable.

I told her that I was queasy, losing vision, and could not feel any of my extremities. She had one of the aids retrieve a

Capri-Sun for me from the cooler. They laid me down as I tried to breathe and regain vision and feeling in my arms and legs. Thank God I was already sitting down during the extractions because I would have for sure lost control and fallen over had I been upright. Even as I type this, I can feel that knot in the back of my throat and my feet are tingling. Someone get me a glass of water, please.

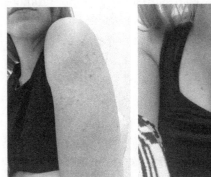

This was the day following that appointment (May 2018).
Sorry you had to see this. Hopefully you weren't just about to sit down for dinner.

That afternoon was harrowing and full of emotion and unfortunately, I still had a long way to go following that consult. It took months for the plan to start to show any progress. The plus side of summer arriving was that the sun tanned me, drying up some of the breakouts and making them less noticeable. Between this and the medication, I was finally starting to gain my confidence back. My boyfriend at the time pointed out that I began sending him selfies again and that he had truly missed them. I had missed them too.

Once fall arrived and I spent less time in the sun and in the ocean, my back and chest began to break out here and there. I was still on the medications that my dermatologist prescribed but the skin on my back had plans of its own. I was starting to lose my mind at this point. I was beyond frustrated. And yes, believe me, I *do* drink enough water. Trust me when I tell you I was doing everything I could to combat this acne. I rarely consumed dairy, gluten, processed sugar, or alcohol. I washed my sheets every two weeks, kept my long hair off my skin, rushed home after every dance class or sweaty workout to cleanse my skin, and I took cold showers so as to not promote the growth of bacteria. I exfoliated, meditated, and got eight hours of sleep every night, yet the acne fought on.

I began seeing an aesthetician to perform "back facials" on me. I had gotten facials on my actual face before and had seen good results, so I did some research to find a place that performed them on the back. Surprisingly, not a lot of places offer this service. They made having my skin poked feel luxurious and I enjoyed going, soon becoming a regular with the same girl who really got to know me and my skin. I did not really have the money to be spending on back facials every month, but the acne disturbed me so greatly that some months I would just swipe the credit card and worry about dealing with it later. I am hopeful that these have contributed to my skin appearing to be a little better, but at the very least, the treatment helps clear current breakouts and reduce the pigmentation of old ones, so I will take what I can get.

Since I am still struggling with pretty severe acne on multiple parts of my body and the antibiotics no longer seem to be working, my dermatologist wants to have me go on Accutane within the next couple months. Initially, I did not want to put Accutane in my body. It seems risky and harmful, requiring monthly blood tests to monitor my health and ensure I do not become pregnant. The medication has been around for a long time, but I would rather not go through the hassle of poisoning my body and taking all of these extreme steps for clear skin. I feel myself fading fast though. My patience thins with each breakout. I am sick of putting plans with new guys on hold because of my skin. I am sick of tearing up when I look in the mirror. I am sick of spending so much money on medication and treatments. I am sick of being self-conscious. I am sick of not wholly enjoying my early twenties because of this.

In recent history, I have had some very clear spells. I have noticed these occur when I am eating very, very cleanly and my stress is low. I am currently dealing with a terrible breakout due to the craziness of moving apartments. I was the clearest I have ever been a couple weeks ago, but the stress of finding a place and then the irregularity of ordering Postmates while in-between stocked pantries was enough for hundreds of pimples to invade my entire back and then down both of my arms again. I was so over being broken out that I engaged in some pretty unhealthy behavior. This is exactly what *not* to do, kids, and if you are a health professional or skin-care professional reading this, I am *so* sorry. Forgive me, I hated my skin *that* much.

When I noticed the severity of this breakout, I began frantically taking double doses of my antibiotics every day. My gut suffered and I will save you the ugly details but safe to say my time in the restroom was *not* pretty. I do not believe in indoor tanning beds—do not go in them, you guys. I am so into preventing premature aging that I wear sunscreen and a hat every time I go outside. I had not used a tanning bed since high school, but I *needed* this breakout covered and dried up so I went to the place I vowed I never would again and purchased a tanning package. I got in for the maximum amount of time (covering my face and hair) in an attempt to kindly scald my skin off.

I booked an appointment with my back facialist for the next day. In the meantime, I was using itchy Retin-A that was prescribed to me on the area. This medication has multiple warning labels against sun exposure on its packaging. It also clearly states to only apply a thin film once a day. Nope, no time for that. I liberally applied this poison day and night. Surprisingly, when I went in for my facial, I was not too sunburned and she wanted to kill my breakout so my lady used some harsh glycolic acid on my skin. Of course, I did not tell her all the abuse I was putting myself through; I wanted her to do her worst! She was concerned when I left that session with some swollen, itchy red patches and gave me some ultra-hydrating cream to help. She had never used that mask on me before so we concluded that it was simply too strong and we probably would not use it again.

The entire session, my skin was stinging and burning but it satisfied me, proving that it was doing its job in absolutely murdering my skin. When I got home, I observed clear, swollen, stinging burns on my arms and back. It was entirely my fault of course, and I honestly was not too bothered. I just applied the lotion to the affected areas and knew it would clear itself up in a few days.

Over the following couple days, I shed enough skin to build my own leather jacket. The burns turned into scabs, which I felt an innate desire to pick at, and the rest of the skin on my arms and back flaked off. I was shocked to find that the pimples were still faintly lingering even after burning a layer of my skin off. The audacity! I went tanning again once the burns were healed. I knew while engaging in these behaviors that they were harmful, but I could not stop myself; I needed to do everything I could to get my clear skin back. I had no more patience to bestow. Maybe at this point it would have just been healthier to plague my liver with Accutane for five months instead.

We have been over the fact that I am a control freak many times already in this book. My acne makes me feel cripplingly out of control because all of the actions I take to prevent it have failed me. This borderline self-abuse was a desperate attempt to control something I simply could not.

I should honestly just title this book *Here's a List of Self-destructive Behaviors I Know Better Than to Engage in But Do Anyway!* Picking. I am addicted to this gross, self-mutilating habit. I engage in picking, scraping, and squeezing my skin even when I do not want to. I find that I pick at my skin more often when areas of my life are in shambles beyond my control. When my skin is mostly clear, I am able to kick the habit almost all of the way, but when it begins to break out, I amplify the damage tenfold by breaking open my skin with my fingers. I am well aware that this only causes the spread of bacteria and ultimately makes breakouts worse, but my experience with picking has led me to conclude that it is an anxious tick of mine.

I remember being at a slumber party in about fourth or fifth grade with girls from my school. We were having a spa day, made up of massages, sticky nail polish, and Aaron Carter tunes blasting in the background. A few of the girls were sitting up close in front of a full-length mirror and showed me how if you squeeze the pores on your nose, gunk comes out. This was an invigorating discovery for me. I would spend many hours in the following years sitting on my bathroom counter at home, digging into my pores. It was never a huge problem that I felt as though I needed to kick until the past few years when my acne got so bad, and I really had to begin to be careful. Now the issue was not just the tiny blackheads on my nose. I had opportunities to pick at my arms, chest, and back. In order for these nauseating infections to disappear, I was going to need to stop.

I need to make sure I am always mindful of where my hands are because if I do not monitor them, they will have made my arms bleed again without me even realizing it. It is a disheartening feeling to realize you have been scratching and picking at your skin for a half an hour while watching television without your knowledge. The only way to combat mindlessness is mindfulness so if I become cognizant of the fact that I have been picking more than usual lately, I will repeat the mantra of my no-more-picking rule over and over again until it sticks. It is a battle against myself.

With my recent breakout, my picking took an intense relapse and I realized it was also parallel to how I was feeling about my body shape at that time. I was struggling in my mind with a couple pounds I had gained and with the acne that had erupted, I felt completely out of control. I was eating healthy and exercising, completely insulted that my body had the audacity to hang onto a few pounds. I also felt betrayed by my skin, breaking out despite all of the precautions I take to prevent acne. Completely out of control in multiple areas of my life, my mind searched for something to do to fix the problems. I am aware that picking at my skin actually breeds the opposite outcome of what I am going for, but some part of me still finds it satisfying. It's as though it is helping the problem get better by purging out my pores.

In addition to my mantra, I incorporate a few other strategies to assist me in breaking this grotesque obsession. I keep my hands and nails as clean as I can and apply fancy lotions to my hands and fingers. If my hands are fresh and sweet, I will not want to empty my pores out onto them so I will resist picking. One time my picking got so compulsive and debilitating that I took my nail clippers and chopped off my beautiful, almond-shaped nails. I cut them down as short as I could and promised myself that when I stopped picking and could have the responsibility of nails again, I could grow them long again.

Additionally, when I can, I also always wear fresh, clean clothes that I am fond of and would not want to get pimple juice all over (gross, I know). Same method is used with my bedding. I have heard that for some people, having their nails always manicured helps too. For me, that works only for like a day. So, unfortunately, it has not proven to be worth the expense.

An investment that does give me good results is getting facials. I have even gotten some professional back facials during the worst of my bacne and had great results; it is hella relaxing too. Hiring someone who is a professional to perform sanitary, safe extractions on my skin has helped me resist the urge to pick tremendously. Knowing I have an appointment coming up that I am spending my hard-earned money on will deter me from performing the duty myself. It also holds me accountable, especially if I see the same aesthetician regularly. She knows my skin and she knows when I have been picking. Self-consciousness is my friend in this situation because I become very timid worrying what she may think when she sees the evidence of my self-inflicted turmoil under her facial lamp.

One of the many reservations that came to my mind when writing this book was that people would think I was pretentious, vain, and guilty of playing the victim card in many areas of my life. I am well aware that there are so many worse problems in the world than acne and parents who love you too much. My problems are first-world, privileged problems I will admit, but writing about them has been therapeutic for me and I hope you have found some things about yourself while reading. If nothing else, at least you got a chuckle out of my pathetic life! Anyway, if acne is something you deal with and if it upsets you the way mine upsets me, know that you are not alone. No one posts photos featuring their pimples on Instagram, and more of us deal with it as adults than you think.

In addition to the facials, what has helped my skin the most is dramatically paying attention to my mental health. The bacteria that form breakouts are produced inside the body so every time I break out, I take a look at what could be going wrong internally. The initial arm flare-up occurred just one month after I began showing symptoms of generalized anxiety disorder. I am no doctor, but I can infer that my hormones went ballistic as a result of my anxiety and this is probably what caused the acne, paired with environmental factors like the polluted air and water in Los Angeles.

It took me about a year of therapy to really feel as though I had begun the healing process from anxiety and my skin certainly seemed to improve as a result. Stressful times laced with cortisol and adrenaline still cause me to break out. In addition to prioritizing the health of my mind, a few other things have helped with my skin. Of course, a low-inflammatory diet has helped; I avoid gluten, dairy, alcohol, and processed sugar when I can. I try not to be too much of a Nazi in this area because as we know, things can get real eating disorder-y for me real quick. Balance is key, remember. I do not cut anything out altogether.

In the book about hormones, *Moody Bitches*, which I have previously noted, the author provides recommendations for a few natural hormone-balancing supplements. I noticed my skin clear up a little bit when I incorporated chasteberry (aka Vitex) capsules and evening of primrose oil capsules (also may help with hormonal migraines) every day. I prefer to stick to natural remedies to avoid screwing with my system too much because it seems as though screwing with our systems can just end up replacing one problem with another. Keeping my anxiety at bay and prioritizing my happiness overall seems to help my skin. It is so interesting to me that when something is wrong, your skin will be the first to tell you. Pay attention to your bodies, people! They are built to be resilient and have evolved over thousands and thousands of years to help us out.

I do realize that I have not made a joke in a while, so if you are asleep, I do sincerely apologize. My acne and anxiety make me feel very out of touch with who I am, and I lose my sense of identity when they are prevalent. I am working on this. My wittiest, most charming self is typically permitted when I feel grounded in the affable, amazing chick I am, so discussing topics that pull me away from her could be to blame for why I am such a bore at the moment. Love you!

The moral of this slightly depressing and cringeworthy chapter is that I want you guys to take good care of yourselves. Life gets really hard even for those of us who seem to have it all. We cannot do it on our own. Seek love from friends and family and seek health care from professionals when you need it. Eat avocados. Meditate. Laugh. Dance. I sometimes feel overwhelmed when I log onto Twitter and read news of another massive tragedy. The amount of bad news we consume daily is detrimental to our health. It is unnatural for me to sit in my Los Angeles home and carry the burden of all the suffering in the world on my own shoulders.

Make your world smaller. This is a concept I love that I heard John Mayer talking about on his Instagram Live talk show, "Current Mood." He pleaded with his audience to shrink its perspective a little bit. We can only do what we can. Recycle, heal yourself first, vote, look around your community to seek ways you can help others, be nice. At times, this is all we can do. I hope to see the world become a better place in my lifetime, but I grow anxious, overwhelmed, and discouraged when I envision all the work that has to be done to get there. We cannot do any of it alone and we cannot do any of it if we do not take care of ourselves first. Do not carry the weight of the world; the weight of your own world is enough for now. Sleep well.

There are a million reasons to live.
Here are some of mine:

_____

_____

_____

_____

_____

_____

_____

_____

_____

_____

_____

_____

_____

_____

_____

I know myself better than anyone else does.
What is my plan of action for when I am feeling down?
What will I do to take care of myself?

My Depression Drive:

_____

_____

_____

_____

_____

_____

_____

_____

_____

_____

_____

_____

_____

_____

_____

Chapter Eleven

Some of You Wash Your Hair Every Day and It Shows

Hello and welcome to my YouTube channel. My name is Rachel! All right, so here I go with a brief chapter of advice. I know I intentionally scalded my skin off one time and thought I had genital herpes for years, but I promise I do also know a thing or two about how to live. Apparently, I must not be a complete mess because friends often seek my opinion on numerous of their life situations. Many of the topics I bring up in this chapter may seem like common sense to you. Trust me, they do to me too, but sometimes when I make these points to friends, they act like I am Gandhi or some shit so I figured it would not hurt to publish them as reminders for all of us.

Here I also narrate another event that I came out of with some major life lessons. Don't be shell-shocked. It's not pretty, but it is a part of my story that needs telling. We all act a little wack sometimes when blinded by the close proximity we have to our own issues so allow me to be the blunt, sometimes painfully honest friend you all need to give you a nice little smack on the back of your head, you crazy little bitch.

Budget your time and money for things that make you truly happy, you broke bitch.

I have always been exceptional with time and money management. I seriously get an endorphin rush from making a checklist, writing out every hour of my upcoming month, or making a spreadsheet of my spending choices. I seriously do not know how people get by without practicing these habits. If you do not have them already, I urge you to order a cute planner (I have two, one for life and one for my personal assisting job) and a notebook off Amazon. Mapping out my plans in these and in the notes section of my phone significantly reduces the clutter in my mind and in turn, lowers stress.

What I really want to get to here though, is this—I find it extremely beneficial to take a moment to budget my time and money in order to make room for the things I really desire in life. I am pretty good about not buying new, on-trend items like AirPods or the latest iPhone. I also try to avoid updating my closet unless there is a stellar piece I am confident will last me a long time. I have been using the same handbag for six years. These sacrifices may be embarrassing for some people, but my point is because of these choices, I was able to go on a trip to Spain with my best friends last year. We reserved decently priced Airbnbs and I caught the cheapest flights I could find. The airline I took to Spain was so cheap, it was borderline concerning. They did not even give us water on our ten-hour flight and the company was shut down months later, but fuck it, I was in Spain, bitch!

If a financial investment is going to bring you joy, you will find a way to make it work. Hell yes, I clip coupons, take advantage of reward programs, and cash-back offers. This is so I can buy that ten-dollar smoothie I love that makes me feel like I can climb Mount Everest.

You can and should do the same planning with your time. Incorporate activities into your everyday routine that make you happy. Do not wait for the weekend; make a nice dinner with your spouse (or dog, if you are me) on a weeknight! Take time off work to leave town. Set your Instagram time limit so you can actually make it to the gym. Remember, you have the same number of hours in a day as Beyoncé, you hoes!

Check your ego and overcommunicate. It is not that big of a deal, you cocky bitch.

You are not that important. That is just the truth. Hey, neither am I, and I wrote a whole book! I often worry that what I say or do is going to affect others more than it ever actually does. I have learned that it is always better to overcommunicate—everyone has survived every time I have. Ask questions that have been on your mind. You may feel dumb in the moment, but once you have asked the question, you will have received your answer and I guarantee the other party involved will likely not even remember the interaction.

Something a friend or significant other is doing is upsetting you? Tell them (ideally in a nicer tone than I am currently using for this chapter). You do not want to hang out with a guy you went on a few dates with again? Let him down easy. I promise he will be okay without you. Going to be late for a meeting? Send a quick phone call that you are on your way. Any time I have been stressed about being late for something and call, the response on the other line is usually something like, "Okay, don't worry. Thanks for letting me know." It is so simple, yet it relieves so much tension for me! Being up front about where I am has been a tool that has always benefitted the people in my life and myself. 10/10 recommend!

Lose the obligation and learn to say no, for fuck's sake.

Usually, I am so wonderful at this one it is nearly comical. This may come as a surprise because of the codependence thing, but somewhere in my development, it must have been ingrained in me that if I do not want to do something, there is no way in hell I am doing it. This applies to conversing with people who do not amuse me, attending birthday parties, and eating vegetables when I was too young to understand the benefits. I was hanging out at a friend's place recently and with a bummed-out look on her face, she informed me that this guy she did not really like might come over. This was puzzling to me so I asked her why the hell she would invite this guy over if she did not want to. Her response included something like, "Well, he's nice, and he fixed my car mirror one time."

I thought, *Fuckin' SO?!* Then I also said this aloud because I am a good friend, guys. It was absolutely astonishing to me that my girlfriend would soil her perfectly serene evening by subjecting herself to the presence of a guy she was not fond of, all out of obligation. Do not do this, you guys. You do not owe anything to anyone, especially if it disrupts your peace.

Ladies and gents, but especially ladies, do not perform sexual acts you do not want to. I know it is hard. This is the one I struggle with the most. When I was in an emotionally abusive relationship in college, that ex created an unwritten rule that I had to suck him off if I was on my period. This led to a temper tantrum from him if I did not feel like performing oral that night. I will admit I submitted a few times just to shut him up. Yikes. Luckily, in my adulthood, I have gotten a little better about communicating in sexual situations and no longer feel guilty about going as far or not far as I want. So yeah, be like adult me. You *do not* have to do anything you do not want to and anyone who gives you shit for being true to yourself can fuck right off.

I know this is shocking news to you guys at this point, but the rumors are true: I am not perfect. I was hesitant to administer any advice in this book because yeah, I drive around for days with my gas light on. I do have really strong instincts, though. I survived college without getting roofied, probably out of mere luck and also because my body typically sends me warning signals to avoid dangerous situations. Being young and a little bit reckless has gotten me into a sticky situation or two, I will not lie. This situation I am about to tell you guys about is more than sticky. I'm sad to say it's dangerous and unnerving. Buckle up. We'll get through it together.

A fun night out in West Hollywood with my friends took a wrong turn after I drank too much tequila. It was "lesbian night" at the gay bars and my friend who is into girls was super pumped that we were all down to go with her for the ride. It was a great night with good music, drinks, and friends. I rarely go out and have been trying to incorporate more balance in my everyday life, so I swallowed my pride, did my hair, and out I went.

Towards the end of the night, a man approached my friend and me to inform me that his "sister" thought I was absolutely gorgeous. My gay gal pal is always teasing me about how I need to try it out with a lady. I knew that as an adult I would like to explore all my options at least once so when this man approached me trying to set me up with his sister on lesbian night, I figured, why not at least meet her? My friend and I sat down at a table with her, another woman, and the man. They had a very relaxed vibe about them and honestly seemed cool. The guy bought my friend and me drinks.

My blood was so saturated with alcohol that I missed the red flag this man revealed to me when he "accidentally" graced my left breast with the back of his hand while "reaching across the table." I remember giving him a weird look and said something like *come on, dude.* He apologized, giggled, and claimed to be gay and solely attracted to men. I laughed it off. Unfortunately, women are all too accustomed to this minor form of sexual assault.

Our new friends informed us that they were going to head back to their place and that we should come over for another drink. They showed us some photos of their house. It looked like one of those Los Angeles pads you see on television. It had a huge open-plan living room, a floating staircase, a zebra painting, a glass table, tall doorways, and one side of the house was completely sealed with glass, overlooking a boxed-in patio that had a pool that lit up different colors. Mind you, I never leave clubs with strangers, and I advise you guys not to, either. My friend who I was with is sometimes bolder than I am in this department and she has some funny stories about shenanigans she has gotten herself into.

I remember sitting at the table thinking we would just accept the drinks, chat for a bit, and then ditch our new friends but my girlfriend thought it would be a fun adventure to go to this "after-party" and we had each other and charged phones so we would be fine. Certainly, nothing could go wrong. I trust my friend and was trying to let my hair down and have more fun in my life. I was also heavily intoxicated, so sure, I thought. Why not? It would be an adventure even though I was not attracted to either of the women or the man we were with.

More red flags that my brain actually was registering at the time—my friend and I got in the car alone with the man and the other two girls got in a separate one. I remember asking him why they were not with us. I do not remember his answer. Guys, I am painfully aware now of how bad this all sounds. I still can't believe I did this. I look back on all of the times I have gotten in random cars with strange men while intoxicated and I worry myself. I know how suspicious it is and I promise I learned my lesson that night and it will never happen again. A lot of my friends and I can recall flirting with danger from time to time and we laugh about all of the stupid shit we have done, especially while drunk, and thank God we have all lived to tell the tales.

When we arrived at the "party," there was no one else there. Luckily the two girls from the bar arrived shortly so it was not just my friend and I alone with this weird guy. The house was stunning. There was a straight-up DJ booth in the living room, dude. It was the perfect setup for a house party. I had never seen anything like it before in person. We chilled, talked, and drank a little more. We watched our new friends do drugs in the bathroom. We smoked cigarettes with them outside, something I have only ever done on a handful of occasions when extremely drunk. It was all fine. I felt safe and relaxed and we were enjoying ourselves. Somehow my friend and I ended up sitting outside with the man and my gay girlfriend, who had been flirting with me all night as she typically does when she is drunk. I do not mind. No pressure, it is all in good fun.

I can't recall what we were talking about, but at some point I agreed to kiss her, so we did a couple times. The man was getting a little pushy, begging us to get in the pool with him. We said no, we did not have bathing suits. Of course he said that was no problem. That was a request we did not give into, thankfully. The three of us were just messing around, laughing outside, and kissing each other for play. I made out with the guy a couple times even though I was not even remotely attracted to him. I have done this before while drunk. Macking on a bunch of random people just for shits and giggles when I am out and single is sort of a pastime of mine that has always been harmless with the exception a few mornings where I awoke with a sore throat, unable to identify the origin.

He and my friend began to grope me and each other. Things took a turn when I began to not enjoy his kisses. I grew kind of grossed out by them, actually. I was okay with messing around with my girlfriend. It was playful and as I mentioned, I trust the shit out of her. We always used to joke about how we would hook up one day.

I can imagine that both of them began to get really into the play even though for me it was strictly fun. I am not really sure how the three of us ended up upstairs. I remember the guy saying he wanted to mess around for a minute and would leave my friend and me shortly. This is all so foggy; my sober brain, of course, has a hard time piecing it all together. The fooling around downstairs was okay with me; it was simple amusement. I do not think that I properly communicated that I did not want it to go any further.

I remember them both all over me in the bed upstairs in a dark room. Honestly, if I had been attracted to the guy, this would have been a dream. I love sexual attention and was receiving a lot of it from both of them. I seriously always fantasized about this type of three-way. It just sucked that the guy sucked. In the moment though, things started to progress beyond my comfort level. My girlfriend was also heavily intoxicated but responded graciously when I rejected any further sexual action. Strictly kissing and messing around was what I was okay with and she could sense that and acted accordingly.

But, all of a sudden, the man's penis somehow came out of his brown khaki pants. I was not sure when or how. I remember him grabbing my hands, forcing me to touch it.

I was not attracted to him; I did not want to. I remember telling him that he should just get himself off in the corner because I did not want any part of it. He became pushier. The next thing I knew, somehow, his penis was in my mouth. I was lying on my back and he was forcing it into my mouth quicker than I could get away. I remember turning my head to the other side when I realized what was happening, but he continued to assault my face with his genitals until he eventually ejaculated in my mouth. I swallowed it and then he abandoned my friend and me in the room. She was adjacent to me but unaware of what was happening due to her own level of intoxication (she hardly remembers any of this and, of course, feels awful). It was dark and I was not screaming or physically fighting back against his advances.

Hindsight is twenty-twenty of course. We should have never gone back to the house with those people. We should never have gone upstairs and I should have gotten up off the bed, left the room, and called an Uber the minute things left the area of plain fun and turned intensely sexual against my will. I do remember verbally objecting to him and I am confident that it was obvious that I did not consent to oral sex. He should have stopped. I know this. My body had frozen. My brain was not able to will me to fight back or simply untangle myself from him and leave the room.

I realize how lucky I was to have never encountered something like that before. I have instructed many men to slow down while hooking up and they had all been so responsive up until that point. Prior to that night, any stranger I was physical with would immediately back off the instant I expressed even a hint of hesitation. I guess that was part of why I did not start screaming or punching when he made unwelcome advances. I assumed he would hear me and listen when I said no.

The next thing I remember after he left the room is waking up, I have no idea how much later. I ran into the bathroom that was attached to the bedroom and dry-heaved over the toilet. I have not thrown up from overconsumption of alcohol since high school so that gives you guys a little more insight about how I never allow myself to get to that level. I woke my friend up, urging her that "we needed to leave." I called an Uber and we went back to my apartment to go back to sleep. One of the definitely not-gay girls saw us leaving as the sun was saying its first, earliest greeting of the day. She told us we did not have to go, that we were welcome to stay and sleepover.

I was not fully cognizant of what happened until images of the night filled my mind the next morning. Disgust, disappointment, and sadness crashed over me like a hundred weighted blankets. While it was happening, it hadn't felt like it was that bad of a night; I enjoyed myself for most of it. There were really only fifteen-twenty minutes that made it all feel sour. I aggressively showered the minute I woke up and once my friend awoke, we giggled about all of the weirdness, but eventually I expressed my hurt and how I felt very violated by the guy. After she made sure I was okay, we parted ways.

I sat in my apartment all day, staring at the wall, feeling numb, witnessing as my mind replayed the night over and over again. Infinite warning signs that I should have recognized exposed themselves to my sober mind. The girls were not gay; the guy was not gay; we got in a car with and accepted alcohol from a stranger. We went to an unfamiliar house in Los Angeles. We hung out there. We kissed him. These were all choices we made. Hi, self-blame. But he should not have preyed upon us; he should not have taken advantage of us; and he definitely should have listened when I told him no. I know all of this. He is the predator at fault here, but of course, I cannot help but kick myself in the shins for everything I should have done differently. I learned my lesson. Never again will I go home with a stranger.

Even though this situation was so shitty, I do realize just how lucky we got. This might be slightly dramatic, but those people absolutely could have murdered us or shipped us off to another country to be trafficked. I feel so fortunate that my friend was with me, that we were able to leave when we did, and I am grateful that he forced himself into my mouth and not my vagina. It could have been so much more horrific. I am shaking imagining the more severe sexual trauma so many women have endured.

What made me feel more at ease that next day was reminding myself that such a situation is avoidable in the future and I am safe now. Luckily, the guy does not have our phone numbers, where we live, or even our last names. I am one hundred percent confident that I will never put myself in that kind of dangerous scenario again, so in a way, I am glad it happened and only resulted in what I am experiencing as manageable damage.

I feel ashamed of the choices I made that nauseating night, although factually, I know I was not the one who did anything wrong. It is hard for me to even admit that I was "assaulted" because some parts of the encounter were in fact consensual. Oftentimes we consent to certain steps, saying "yes" to going home with someone, getting in bed with them, even beginning to engage in sexual intercourse. But we always have the right to say no, at any point. There are likely people reading this who have been through something like this—consenting "yes" until they said "no."

No matter what has occurred before that "no," it must stop there. We feel guilty for saying "no" because of previous "yesses," but anyone with a brain can hear you when you say no and they must immediately respect your choice. I know other women have had it so much worse than I and that truth brings tears to my eyes and causes me to question whether or not I should even write about this incident. Let's talk more often about these blurred lines, shall we?

So, it really only takes one unsolicited cock in your mouth to really fuck you up, huh. I wanted to write about it because I learned so many valuable lessons that night and also, of course, because writing has become my outlet and a way for me to shock-absorb my challenges in life. The morning after that sickening night in early spring, my initial reaction was to stuff it down like any other bad hookup and ignore the reality of what had occurred. The guy was repulsive to me. The thought of him violating my body in the way he did caused me to wince and still does to this day. The image and feeling of his penis in my mouth kept making an unwarranted appearance in my head. Haunting stills of that dark room kept coming back.

It is insane how when you experience flashbacks of a dramatic event, all of the feelings, sensations, and smells come right along with it. I experienced crying spells and grew anxious in the days following the incident. I could hardly eat. The taste of Red Bull and his semen kept returning to me. I developed a habit of nervously brushing my teeth, swishing strong mouthwash, and compulsively chewing gum just to taste something else.

The day following the assault, I had a laser hair-removal appointment. I recall feeling slightly triggered undressing in front of two strangers less than twenty-four hours after the event, but the women who administered my treatment that day were incredible. I appreciated the seemingly minor actions they took to ensure my comfort. In previous visits, I had not noticed the way they continually informed me where they were going with the laser, checked in with me to see how I was doing, asked if they needed to slow down, and encouraged me that I was a champ. These minute gestures by these women at the med spa helped me begin to feel in control and gain ownership of my body again on that paper-lined, padded table in that tiny pink room.

I confided in my best friends and eventually in my therapist once I realized that suppressing the emotions around this cringeworthy incident had the potential to cause permanent damage. I cried, mourning the carefree woman I was before that night, but I was determined to get her back. I would not give that asshole the power to take anything more from me. I cannot fathom not being able to discuss this with my best friend, a mental health professional, and hell, you guys. If you have been through anything even the slightest bit traumatic, I encourage you to reflect on it, feel it, talk about it, and let yourself heal despite the grotesque pain that is paired with the process. You got this.

Aside from the safety precautions I will absolutely practice in order to ensure it never happens again, I have also learned a lot about coping with trauma. In the days following the incident, I worried that future sexual encounters might be triggering. I feared that my kinks would change and that I would no longer enjoy being dominated by men the way I once did. My mind dwelled on those terrible fifteen or so minutes rather than remembering how wonderful the rest of the night (and my life) had been.

When I phoned my best friend for comfort, the mantra she repeated to me over and over was that I was no longer in danger. *I was safe now.* Even though my body had exited that dark bedroom, my mind had not. I felt scared even though I was double-bolt locked in my apartment with my sixty-pound

German Shepherd mutt. Any time I experience a flashback or get a whiff of Red Bull, I remind myself *I am safe now.*

Additionally, I have spent a lot more time meditating in order to calm myself down. Breathing, talking about it, and acknowledging where I am in the present moment (which is *not* in that dark room, on that bed, with that awful man) has helped me significantly. Again, my case feels mild and I emerged alive and with no physical injuries. I urge anyone who has withstood any type of assault to seek help from a mental health professional. If I experienced emotional turmoil as a result of my incident, I cannot even fathom what some of you have gone through. It is so essential that we unpack our demons and not let them live inside of our minds. I am aching with awareness that it is not always easy to ask for help or to even speak of the darkest times of our lives. To all of the survivors out there, I witness your strength and stand in awe of you.

One of the hardest components of all of this was accepting the hard, blatant truth that I am not perfect. I made some mistakes and unintentionally burned myself as a result. But I still deserve my own forgiveness. Even though I was reckless that night, I did nothing to deserve ignorance of my requests. I did nothing to deserve to have my body be taken advantage of. Nobody deserves that. Love you.

Get seven to nine hours of sleep every night. I will fight you!

So it turns out that one of the biggest threats to our health as a society is sleep deprivation. Yes, it is equally as important as diet and exercise so treat it that way, you tired bitch. I heard about some recent studies on an episode of the Joe Rogan Experience (JRE) that showed the dramatic effects of losing sleep like obesity, mental illness, cancer, heart disease, and more. You should go take a listen. It will motivate you to get your shit together in the bedroom. I am too lazy to go back and reiterate all of the wonderful stats discussed in the interview that caused me to implement such great changes.

I now prioritize sleep as a need in my life and the effects have been wondrous. And no, I do not care when my friends make fun of me for leaving places early. Grandma is *not* trying to be depressed tomorrow, so tease all you want. My mood is better. I am happier, I eat healthier, and my athletic performance has improved. I did my homework, now it is your turn. I will provide the title of the JRE episode in the back of this book. In *Moody Bitches*, Holland mentions that during daylight savings time, the number of clients seeking therapy for depression significantly increases, so yes, that single hour really does make a difference. Sleep is the shit. Get on it. You are welcome.

Be a bold bitch.

You must take risks. Playing it safe is selling yourself short and you WILL regret it. Go after your dreams, audition, tell your crush you think they are cute, dare to make life better for yourself. You literally have nothing to lose. It is so simple, you guys.

Breathe and slow down, you busy bitch!

This one is pretty self-explanatory. Also, I am tired and need to slow down too. Basically, take it easy and do not rush through life. The world is not going anywhere. Yes, work your ass off to make your dreams come true but also realize that things take time. You have time to take a half day so you can go drive to the beach. You have time to sit down on a pillow for five minutes and meditate every morning. Take a breath with me, bitch.

Be a nice bitch.

This one also speaks for itself. I find that being kind to strangers and not-strangers improves my day-to-day mood immensely. It also feeds my ego and is extremely satisfying when someone is a straight cunt to me because of their own issues and I reply in a sweet, relaxed tone. I like to take a moment in the early hours of my day to make the choice that I am going to be pleasant today because I will admit that I can be a nightmare sometimes. When I make that decision, it holds me accountable to smile at strangers, be extra gracious to people who are working in customer service, and really listen when people are talking to me. It is true what they say—it costs zero dollars to be nice. It is the least we can do for ourselves and the tense world around us. Also, do not sleep with someone's boyfriend. Just don't. Hashtag positivity!

Educate ya damn self.

The current political climate is incredibly messy. Mass shootings are an epidemic. Women's rights, LGBTQ rights, and minority rights are being threatened. It is not difficult to feel helpless if you cannot afford donations to Planned Parenthood or the ACLU and when elections only come around every couple years. My advice is to press on. Speak out for what you believe in and ask for more from your leaders. I completed *The Body Keeps the Score* around the time abortion bans were being passed in multiple states and it was clear that some political leaders were attempting to overturn Roe v. Wade. The epilogue of this book about trauma is so beautiful. Van der Kolk calls readers to open their eyes to the effects of trauma on our society, where it comes from, and how to stop it before it occurs. Tears ran down my face reading this. I wished I could provide a safe home and great education for the underprivileged children in our society, painfully aware that this would solve so many of our nation's issues.

> I wish I could separate trauma from politics, but as long as we continue to live in denial and treat only trauma while ignoring its origins, we are bound to fail. In today's world, your ZIP code, even more than your genetic code, determines whether you will lead a safe and healthy life. People's income, family structure, housing, employment, and educational opportunities not only affect their risk of developing traumatic stress but also their access to effective help to address it. Poverty, unemployment, inferior schools, social isolation, widespread availability of guns, and substandard housing all are breeding grounds for trauma. Trauma breeds further trauma; hurt people hurt other people.
>
> – Bessel Van der Kolk, *The Body Keeps the Score*

Trauma breeds trauma. Hurt people hurt people. If you are a school educator, watch over those children; ask them about their lives. Public defenders and social workers of the world, I see you doing wonderful things. Politicians who genuinely care about their people, not just money—keep fighting the good fight. We love you. Everyone should read *The Body Keeps the Score*, even if you have not experienced what you may think of as textbook trauma. It educated me on the breeding grounds of abuse and I am more empathetic to numerous mental conditions and am even better equipped to look out for my fellow humans as a result of this information.

You are allowed to be a mess. Take that from one of the shittiest of shit shows you know, me! Life is hard and it certainly puts us through a lot of bullshit. You can and should feel the effects of the trials and tribulations of this roller coaster we are riding. Listen here, though, people. What you are not allowed to do is cause catastrophic damage everywhere you go due to your own unresolved issues. Go to therapy when a relationship ends, when a relationship begins, when someone dies, when your work life is unsatisfactory, when you are thinking about having a child, when it's winter, when it's summer (you get the point I am trying to make here, right?). It is the responsible thing to do. Part of being an adult and contributing kindness out into the world is having the self-awareness to acknowledge and battle your own faults. No one is perfect, but we can all reduce our asshole footprint on the earth by digging deep within ourselves.

I pride myself on my ability to communicate my messiness. When I was fresh out of my breakup with Tyler and I went on a date with a new guy, I immediately informed him of my situation and that I was not ready for anything serious. I was in pieces on the inside but there was no way in hell I was going to use others and tear them down because of it. Time and time again, men have come my way while licking their wounds. Sure, I do accept fault for allowing them into my lives, but honestly, they are grown men who should gain a sense of control over themselves. The pain these types of people have caused me and so many others in the past is due to their lack of self-awareness, communication skills, and possibly their lack of ability to care about anyone but themselves. No bueno.

Do the noble thing and do your best to piece yourself back together. Your current and future relationships will be better because of it, if you choose; your children will be happier because of it; and so will you. Stop being lazy and work on your damn self. I know it is scary and uncomfortable. Grow up.

Stop chasing the wrong things, beeotch.

So there are a few key things that I consider to be some hot secrets to happiness. Some of them are easy, some of them are not. Of course I consider meditation to be one of the easiest ways to feel happier overall in your everyday life. But a large-scale, long-term issue I have been noticing in the world around me is the way we are setting ourselves up for unhappiness by chasing the wrong things, hoping they will be the answer to all of our issues.

This clicked for me recently when someone I knew went on a new diet. Something to know about this person is that they are just one of those people who is usually in a bad mood. I am not experiencing their life, so I truly do not know if they are happy deep down, but it seems as though they are never satisfied and always have something to complain about. We all know these people who are just bummers, right? Anyways, with their new regimen, people all around us were giving compliments and this person was accomplishing the physical goals they had set for themselves. But did their overall aura of negativity change? Nope. Were they still the same seemingly miserable person as before? Yup.

So yeah, it was then when my eyes were opened to so many of us chasing the wrong things and then failing over and over again to find happiness. I am not just speaking from my experience as a witness to this pattern in others but also as a perpetuator of it firsthand. I cannot tell you the number of diets I have gone on expecting to be a new, happier person once those five pounds were gone. Once they were, guess what? I wanted to lose five more and I still did not like my body.

We chase romantic relationships, fantasizing about being in love and how having a wonderful partner will suddenly fix our entire life. I even do this today, but in order to ground myself and stay present, I remind myself that even when I did have a great boyfriend, I still had panic attacks. We chase material items, money, and higher social status but forget that these are empty and cold. We convince ourselves that once we get that promotion or book our dream gig, our lives will be perfect.

Of course we need a handful of things to keep us alive and well. We need our health, a roof over our heads, people who love us, and a job that provides us with purpose. If you are reading this, I am assuming you are able to make your next rent payment somehow or another. It is also extraordinary, crucial even, to set goals and work hard to attain what you want out of life. But do not think for a second that once you reach your goal, you will be perfectly happy all of a sudden. The point I am trying to make here is focused on when we pursue the nonessentials in order to find happiness, only to find that we went wrong somewhere in our pursuits and now we're crying alone on our bathroom floor.

When I got signed with my dance agent (a lifelong goal of mine), I did not feel satiated. I had a hard time enjoying the last cool dance gig I had worked because my eating disorder was consuming my mind. When I was hanging out with the celebrity crush I had for years, I was still unhappy in my everyday life. When I was ten pounds lighter and receiving tons of positive feedback for how good I looked, I was miserable. When my skin cleared up after two years of embarrassing breakouts, guess what? Still sad.

Spoiler alert, our lives will never be perfect, but here is the good news: we can be happy anyway. We can work towards improving our lives, but we can also find peace along the way. We have to. Because if we are not happy now, we will not be happy then. I know I am not the first to say it, but I also know we (you and I) need all the reminders we can get. I want us all to take a deep, hard look inward. It is not going to be comfortable, pretty, or glamorous. It is going to be painful, messy, and gross. Sit with yourself on those lonely days and question why, *truly* why you are not happy. Stop distracting yourself by overbooking your schedule, turning to social media, sex, drugs, food, and television. Everywhere I look, people are numbing their pain with these temporary coping mechanisms. But at the end of the day, no matter how far you run, you still have to bring your mind with you when you run. You may as well make it a safe place to reside.

By meditating, talking shit out for a countless number of hours on my therapist's couch, reading self-help books, spending a ton of time alone, and writing this damn book, the unaddressed discrepancies in my approach to life thus far began to reveal themselves. I had to fix my relationship with my body and with food because it was wounded. I had to stop giving too much of myself to other people. I had to learn to be comfortable with, accept, and eventually come to adore my intense emotions. I had to learn how to be my own advocate. I had to learn how to surrender control and have faith. I had to learn how to trust myself. I did the work. Now it is your turn.

So, why are you unhappy? I will save you the suspense. It is not because you don't have abs, it is not because you are single, and it is not because you cannot afford the new Yeezys.

It is likely because there is an imbalance somewhere—in the way you see the world, in the way you see yourself, the way you see the timeline of your career. Unfortunately, I can't tell you exactly why you are unsatisfied with your life as much as my codependent brain is screaming that I have the answers and is begging me to save you all. It is time for you to do your homework and shift your perspective, kiddos! Let me know how it goes.

And finally, vote, drink water, take your omega-3s, wear sunscreen, and stop washing your hair every day, you crusty bitch!

Let's start chasing the right things by getting to the
bottom of this.
Why am I actually unhappy?

_____

_____

_____

_____

_____

_____

_____

Okay, now get up off your ass. It's go time.
What am I going to do about it?

_____

_____

_____

_____

_____

_____

_____

Chapter Twelve
Let's Go Buffalo

Do you ever take the time to pair your phone's Bluetooth with your car, go to your Spotify's search bar, type in that song you have been so sweetly craving for hours, press play, and blast the volume only to zone out the whole time or get distracted by road rage and miss the greatness? The track dances its final chorus and all of a sudden you wake up wondering where that stunning intro and all the verses went.

Yeah, I wanted to flex about my car being made in 2014 and having Bluetooth capabilities, but I also wanted to outline my struggles with remaining present and ultimately resorting to nostalgia in the simplest way possible. To me, the feeling I get when that song ends and I did not even notice my favorite parts is the easiest way to describe how I feel when I have let beautiful moments in life pass me by, unacknowledged, while living them. If my time on this earth has taught me one thing, it is that everything is temporary. The only thing constant is change—all that jazz, yada yada. No one hates an overused cliché more than ya girl, but I am so sorry, my dudes, that one is true. And it is painful. Often when a period of time ends, we did not see it coming. Or if we did, we did not anticipate how we would actually feel when that ending arrived.

My friends, do you ever lie in bed at night reminiscing about that one time you sat on a balcony overlooking the Mediterranean Sea, laughing and drinking wine with your soul mates? I sure do. Do you ever recall how it felt to wake up next to the deepest, purest love you have ever been in? What it would feel like to stuff your face into that person's neck one more time and take a big giant inhale? I do. Do you sometimes wish you could smack your younger self in a certain situation and shout, "Bitch! Do you see what is happening right now? Open your eyes! Be present! Girl!?" I sure as hell do.

Over time, I have learned that this is one of the coolest characteristics about these moments, though. When you are in them, you are unaware of how colossal they are and how you will someday be crying laughing, telling your friends about them.

I am certainly not the master of being present; oftentimes you can find me looking forward to the next thing on my agenda. I am currently trying to incorporate the importance of taking a couple extra breaths every now and then. Whenever I have a friend who is in a new relationship and she is giddy with dopamine, I urge her to drink that shit all the way in, honey. I nag her about it over and over again. As a feelings addict, love—specifically hyper-charged new love—is one of my favorite strains of my drug. I am not saying you and your boyfriend are going to break up, but feelings do change over time, so if you like where you are right now, *enjoy it*. It will likely evolve into something that is rich and beautiful too, but it will be different, that is all.

If you look around at your life and cannot seem to locate something to appreciate, imagine how different your life may be in five years. Will you be living in the same place? Be around the same people? Have the same pet? I guarantee something will change, so if there is anything at all that you like about today, I urge you to drink that motherfucker, swirl it around in your mouth, and gargle it before you swallow.

As comforting as it is for me to mosey around and be nostalgic, overromanticize the past, and feel bad for myself, I have an inclination that all of this reminiscing I've become so good at could be trying to tell me something. Gosh, being self-aware is exhausting work! Can't I just have *one night* to cry myself to sleep wishing I could tell my ex who I am convinced is one of my soul mates that his mouth breathing is in fact adorable?! I am addicted to feelings, and feelings are fleeting moments that always end. So where do we go from here, then?

It is easy for me to pound away at this keyboard while currently lonely as hell and single as fuck and promise myself that the next time I find love, I will savor it like it is the last piece of apple pie on earth when we all know for damn certain that I would shove that slice down my throat quicker than you could say, "Do you want ice cream with that?"

Nothing is compartmentalized, my dudes. I will say it again—the way we do one thing is the way we do everything. I need to stop leeching on love as if it were my last meal. I need to stop leeching on meals as if they were my last meal. I experience these relationships, vacations, years of my life, and desserts as if I am prancing around through a daisy field, head in the clouds, and then BAM, all of a sudden, I have run straight through a black tunnel and been catapulted out to the other side alone, wondering when my plate emptied.

From here on out, when high on a sensation, I invite both you and me to attempt to look at the current moment as if it had already gone. Zoom out. Let us try to imagine how our future selves would view our current selves and proceed to enjoy the moment as if it were a treasured memory we were desperately longing for while in bed alone after drinking too many glasses of Pinot Noir.

So I talked about nostalgia, change, and being in the present moment. Now I want to discuss soul mates. I know what you are thinking. This chapter makes you worry I would be more fit wearing white gaucho pants, dancing barefoot on some beach, wearing a necklace made of rocks. I am a pessimist, but I am also a hopeless romantic, I cannot help myself. The same part of my brain that believes I am fiery and passionate because of where the planets were the moment I was born also believes there are souls we are destined to encounter in this batshit crazy world.

Soul mates are a part of our being from the second we begin to breathe the air of this earth. Soul mates carry us with them too. They challenge us, grow us, and make us better versions of ourselves. When I talk about soul mates, I am talking about the people we happen to stumble upon that have the greatest impact on our lives. You could be in a relationship with one for your entire life, or only for a brief period of time. But it was all meant to be.

Two of my soul mates are my girlfriends I have had since I was twelve years old. Lindsey, my soul mate, is as brilliant and hilarious as she is beautiful. It is annoying, really. You would all be gravely jealous of her long legs, blonde hair, and cinematically large blue eyes, I just know it! I am so unbelievably blessed to have this fine wine of a woman in my life. We met in middle school and were notorious for giggling too much in class. We would create ridiculous scenarios in our heads and laugh at them until we cried. I specifically remember one that brought us to tears in the seventh grade. We thought it would just be the funniest damn thing ever to walk into McDonald's and ask for items they did not have on their menu. Eyes crossed and with a stupid voice, of course. "CAN I HAVE SPAGHETTI AND MEATBALLS, PLEASE?!" So dumb but so silly to us at that age. I am laughing as I write this.

Before we were old enough to drive, we would fill the days by venturing on long walks through our neighborhoods, taking goofy photos on a playground with our digital cameras, and stealing beer from the local country club's abandoned golf carts. Lindsey brings much needed laughter, joy, and lightheartedness to my world. To this day, you can still find us getting a kick out of playing with Snapchat filters for hours or peeing our pants howling at our fake Instagram accounts. I always have the time of my life when I am with her. We were the epitome of troublemakers in high school. Do not get me wrong; we both did exceptionally well academically, but we definitely spent a weekend or fifty riding around in cars with strange guys just to smoke some weed or sneaking out to parties with our older boyfriends. The best part of those nights was returning home buzzed, raiding the pantry, and laughing together on random subjects.

The past ten-plus years with her have been like a magical, sentimental dream that you only see on movie screens. It is so special to look back on all of those times that were crucial to shaping who I am and see her by my side, smiling, laughing, and dancing. After we graduated high school, we attended the same college where we even got to share an apartment for a semester. We have travelled to Europe multiple times as a unit; the list of incredible memories is extensive considering we are both still in our early twenties.

In addition to endless laughs, Lindsey has always been around to be a spine of stability for me. She is an impeccable leader and has an impressive marketing career to show for it. She holds my artist brain steady and uses logic to rationalize situations where I tend to be overly emotional. We are both strong personalities, but we complement each other just like chicken wings and pizza.

I have always admired the way Lindsey goes about her life. She never lets tough things get to her and she has her eyes on the prize at all times. Her logic allows her to live life the way I believe it should be lived: simply. She wants to have a fun weekend? She will make sure it happens. No questions asked. She wants to get a golden retriever puppy? No ifs, ands, or buts, it is done. She is in love? She makes the relationship work. It has been the privilege of my life to watch her evolve into the powerful woman she is today. She is loyal to her friends and family while working hard for what she wants and never compromising. We could all take a note or two from my soul mate. Goddamn, am I one lucky girl?!

Samantha is the essential third of my entire heart that is this small group of us soul mates. My relationship with this woman is the one that made me believe soul mates were real. Our friendship has grown and blossomed beautifully throughout the years, stronger each day. I only surround myself with the best of people, clearly, because similar to Lindsey, Samantha makes me laugh until I cry and helps me look inward, making me a better person.

She is one of my biggest cheerleaders and I have her to thank for a lot of the self-confidence I have developed. If I ever feel down on myself, I look at myself through her eyes, remembering her words of affirmation that she has written to me on numerous birthday cards and voiced to me over long phone calls. I have answered the phone to her sobbing over a breakup and months later, when it was my turn, hers was the first number I dialed after I hung up on my relationship. (Let's be real. I went in my contacts and clicked on her name. It is 2019, for Christ's sake, but *dialed* just sounds cooler.) We talk on the phone for three hours almost every week and never run out of things to say. Both of us are obsessed with bettering ourselves so we go on and on about our latest discoveries.

We are pure soul mates in the sense that we are best friends; being around each other is comfortable, fun, and natural. But what truly makes us soul mates is the way we learn from one another. It is difficult for me to define the way we effortlessly understand each other and exactly why, so that causes me to resort to otherworldly terms like soul mate. Ninety-nine percent of the time, she knows what I am thinking without me having to say a word and vice versa. I hope for all of humanity to find a soul mate like mine; a love so true it can withstand the test of time, change, and distance. We live on opposite sides of the country at the moment so when we do get to spend time together, we cherish it like a precious diamond or an ice-cream sandwich on a summer day. I recall being home for the holidays last year, going crazy in my own mind due to too much family time, and being knocked off my LA routine. I waited patiently for her to be done with work so I could complain on her couch or go to a yoga class with her to vinyasa my sanity back.

When I recall my moments with Sam, I think of laughter at the stories from our lives that we push over the edge with ridiculous antics. Our humor plays off one another and we love taking things too far. We can go from giggling about a comical one-night stand to crying about childhood trauma. It is seamless and effortless—a true testament to how synchronized our wavelengths are.

It is safe to conclude that my Sammy has not had life handed to her on a silver platter. She has faced challenges with relationships, family, school, work, and her mental health. Her open-mindedness, strength, positive attitude, and ability to fight through dark times endlessly inspires me. For her, there is no other option other than to carry on and push through challenges without a complaint. Most of the time, she is too tough on herself by constantly focusing on ways she can improve, and at times doesn't give herself enough credit for all that she is. Sammy, if you are reading this, know that you are the warrior goddess of my universe and the half that makes me whole. I would not be who I am without you.

Life has changed for all of us in so many ways over the years. Graduations, boyfriends, new cities, new jobs, new pets, deaths, vacations, hair colors, and so on. When I look around myself, disoriented, desperately searching for some form of consistency to grasp onto, they are there. Over the years, they have become my family, unfailing in their presence. Sometimes I cannot think of what I could have possibly done to deserve such loyal, loving sidekicks. My eyes well up imagining the years' worth of memories that we have underneath our belts and I look forward with joy to more that will come. I find solace knowing I will be okay no matter what because I will always have them.

The way some people dream of spending happily ever after with a romantic partner, I dream of us all growing old in the same town, our children and dogs all inseparable companions, abandoning our husbands on weekends for wine and laughter-filled getaways. Sammy and I joke that we will live together in a giant house, unmarried, having our sexy young male lovers over when the nights grow lonely. Lindsey is invited too, but it is appearing as though she and her boyfriend of the past four years (who has also become family) will end up together and reside in a neighboring home, shaking their heads at our cougar lifestyles.

I cannot stress this enough: they are both so incredibly brilliant and have wonderful stories of their own to tell. I do not think it is irrational to advise you to be on the lookout for their books someday in the future.

Romantic Soul Mates

Come on, you guys know by now how much of a sap I am. You had to know this was coming. This chapter is full of clichés with no end in sight, my dudes. But you know what? There is a reason that clichéd sayings are overused. Typically, there is evidence as to why we all repeat these lines over and over again in conversation. It is because there is truth, meaning, and longevity to back them up. Similar to platonic soul mates, I believe we can have multiple romantic soul mates in our lifetimes. I hate to break it to you, sis, but not every guy you date is your soul mate. You can learn from a relationship and even have been destined to meet that person for some particular reason the universe only knows but still have that person not be your destined soul mate.

From all of my romantic relationships thus far, I have gained knowledge about myself and the world around me, but I only suspect that I have encountered one romantic soul mate thus far. I am reluctant to even include this bit in my book for the sake of turning it into a romance novel that I know you guys did not sign up for. I will keep it brief for ya.

Romantic relationships are messy and complicated and sometimes impossible to sustain over long periods of time because of all the different factors that go into nurturing them. To me, a romantic soul mate does not always mean that you are going to live happily ever after with that person. It does mean, though, that your beings were meant to encounter one another at some point in your lives. When you meet, an ease encompasses the soul knowing it recognizes one of its own kind. You were cut from the same cloth. I have already talked about someone I believe to be one of my romantic soul mates at length in this book so you can all take a wild guess and likely infer correctly.

Yep, it's Tyler. I have opened up to you about the ways I learned from him and the simple, yet deep way we love and understand each other. From the moment we met, I was intrigued by him. It was a sunny July day, and a lake and sky were our backdrop, just like a painting. When Tyler found his way next to me, my body instantly lit up. I could not breathe, but at the same time, I felt as though I was inhaling oxygen for the first time in my life. Do not make fun of me; I am an artist, you guys!

There were obstacles that presented themselves, many reasons on paper that we probably should not have pursued each other, but we did anyway. We were helpless, face-to-face against the laws of nature. Seeing him again was effortless. Falling in love with him was effortless. It felt like it would never end. Loving him was one of the most intense, intoxicating feelings I have ever felt. Our partnership and unity felt as though it was written on the stars and manufactured in our cells. Who knows if we will end up together or even see each other again, but I carry a piece of him wherever I go and he does the same with me.

I look forward to future soul mates, knowing the electricity and peace they have the potential bring into my life. If you are trying to date me and you have read this far, first of all, WHY? You saw those photos of my acne, did you not? Second, I do not think you need to be intimidated by the way I write about my ex. I do get all warm, fuzzy, and poetic, but I am a firm belieber (that was a typo, but I think I am going to keep it) that life runs its course and I am exactly where I need to be at the moment, which could very possibly be single AF. So hit me up, hotties! We all have shit in our closets; I am just awesome at being a chronic over sharer. Don't be jealous, ladies!

Here's To You, Dreams

So if you harbor enough humility in your bones and were able to swallow your pride to spend this length of your valuable time consuming the banter of a twenty-three-year-old, I appreciate your loyalty and applaud your optimism.

I want to share a little bit with you about where I found the inspiration to write this book. Predictable, I know, but when I went through my breakup with Tyler, I began spending a maddening amount of time gazing inwards. A few months after the breakup, I traveled to my hometown for the holidays. Flying across the country with my rescue dog for the first time, residing in my childhood home, spending time around family for the first time since ending my relationship with my ex of two and a half years, and struggling with an eating disorder during holidays was a little too overwhelming for me to handle all at once.

So, what did I turn to? Nope, not a healthy outlet like therapy, yoga, reading, writing, or talking it out with the people who cared about me. I brought my case to the internet, of course! There is something so soothing to me about blindly barking to my Twitter followers about my mental health issues. It feels anonymous in some way despite having my full name listed on every tweet. I dreamed that maybe someone would see my one-liners and giggle or even find it in them to relate, when honestly, they were more likely to be rolling their eyes behind their phone screens and heading towards the unfollow button as diligently as they could.

Suddenly, my Snapchat persona turned into that of a self-deprecating, emotional wreck who had a knack for making humor out of the darkest parts of her psyche. I was almost positive that people were merely tolerating my anecdotes, clicking through, disappointed that it was yet again, not a picture of my boobs. Side note: I think that is why most straight men follow me, just scraping by with the modest glimmer of hope that I might accidentally post one of my nudes. You can imagine their disappointment when I hopped on my Snapchat story to address my eating disorder.

Anyway, I began using humor to accompany some tough moments. Over the months to come, I documented my dating app experiences, mental epiphanies, and goofy speculations for my hundred or so Snapchat friends to see, or to ignore. Since Snapchat archives stories, I am allowed to go back and view everything that I have previously posted. In February (the breakup was in September and the cray-cray Snapchat personality began shortly after), I was milling through my library of Snap stories and became extremely intrigued by what I had posted. I had mindlessly authored a flipbook of my own thoughts. I was utilizing Snapchat to capture the evolution of my personal self-discovery. It was impeccable for me to go back and see where my mind was at in such sporadic moments over the recent past. I also fancied myself a laugh or two with my self-reflective comedy. Maybe it was pure narcissism, but I thought to myself, *I might actually have something going here.*

As I continued producing this format of content, a handful of friends would respond to my stories here and there, saying things like "OMG, I LIVE for these." This, of course, nourished my ego even more, but it also gave me a tiny sense of validation that my instinct that I had created something unique and valuable was not utterly insane. Recently, I posted a more lengthy, detailed story about an aha moment I had regarding my masochism. Following that post, a friend sent me a message confiding in me that over the past few months, my stories had not only made her LOL, but they also assisted her in working on her own mental health struggles. You read that right: *my Snapchat stories* helped a friend cope with legitimate issues she was facing. "Wow" was all I could say and yes, I unequivocally cried. Come on, you know me by now!

That same day, an acquaintance from high school, one of the smartest people I know, by the way, a Cornell Law School grad who I have faith will be a member of Congress by the time this book gets published, appraised me that she cherished my stories and that they were like secondhand therapy for her. These testimonials opened my eyes to the case that this was an odd talent I had manufactured without even realizing it. Even if it was just two people, at the very least, I was entertaining someone, and they were identifying with the content.

Where do I go from here? I thought. I did not want to start a blog because blahhhh, boring, and no one actually reads blogs anyway, right? My life is not nearly impressive enough for me to dramatize it into some sort of sitcom or Broadway musical. Everyone would fall right asleep. Podcasts seem to be the hottest platform for millennials to use these days, but I required a medium that I could edit and filter, just like my Snap stories. I already regret half the things that come out of my mouth, so it is going to be a *hard pass* on hours of rambling into a microphone for the world to evaluate and criticize, thank you! We should all take a moment to be appreciative that I am granted the ability to delete old tweets after reflecting for a second.

I never thought I would write a book. I have never considered myself to be a writer, but I began to jot down some of my favorite Snapchat story captions as if they were chapter titles and before I knew it, I was using them to outline subjects of my life. There have been a million moments of self-doubt throughout this operation. Never in a lifetime did I trust I would be able to do this. When I was approximately eight thousand words in, I googled the average book word count and laughed out loud. Some nights, I abandoned my laptop, believing I had nothing remaining to preach, but I always woke up the next morning with fresh words and ideas floating around in my head.

Parallel to the minor compound of my subconscious that screamed I could never actually have the dance career I wanted, a little devil has been sitting on my shoulder, taunting me as I park a seat at my laptop with my glass of wine. It whines, "You will never have enough to say to complete a whole book. If you write this, no one will read it and the ones who do will think it is mediocre, useless, and perpetually unfunny."

I have dedicated this book to my social media friends because while this ghost was trying to get me to quit, you all pressed me to venture on. You all assured me that I used humor in a marketable way and that you looked forward to hearing what I had to say. Say you are not one of those people who encouraged me and are seething with anger and resentment that I have comprehensively wasted your time, I will forward their contact information to you and you can email them directly with any complaints you may have.

I am confident in the conclusion that I have never been the smartest or the funniest person in the room at any given time. Even if it is just my dog and I in my studio apartment, she still takes the cake. Growing up, so much of my value was placed on my looks because that was primarily what the world granted me attention for. No one really asked for my advice or picked my brain for my assessments. Of course, my parents thought I was intelligent and witty, but they made me, they had to. The truth is, the handful of people who informed me that my Snapchat stories aided them through formidable stages inspired me to write this, but if I am being completely honest, it was a mostly selfish feat even if I did not realize it at first.

I have had equally as many revelations while composing this book as I have experienced in years of therapy. Words and concepts I had not previously conceived of spilled out of my mind as I typed these pages. This book has helped me make sense of it all and you better believe I am crying right now! I have found myself hypnotized among these sentences, levitating from my chair for hours on end, generating a divine, healing form of therapy and meditation for me. The first few days of writing this book, I did not track one calorie, and that was coming off six months of restricting. I ate cheese and drank wine like I vowed I would. I listened to my body. I stayed up late.

Writing this has prevented me from texting my ex, fawning over what Adrenaline Guy might think of me, and has distracted me, thereby saving me from the guilt of missing a workout while having the flu. This book has rescued me from the pitfalls of my own mind.

I never thought I could write a book. When I started to, I never thought anyone would read it and so to you, I am immeasurably honored. In the beginning stages, I always prefaced telling people I was writing a book by saying, "Hey, this is going to sound crazy, but …" or "yeah, it is mostly just for me, but I've been writing a lot lately" out of fear of rejection. It baffles me how many people responded to this with blank expressions on their faces, replying with "of course you are writing a book, Rachel. I always knew you would." This blew my mind.

To all the friends who proofread and informed me that they were on the edge of their seat anticipating more, I could not have done this without you. Thank you, reader for riding the roller coaster that is my mind with me, it has been a joy taking you along. I hope you have discovered a piece or two about your own inner demons as well.

If you collect nothing else from this, please hear me when I tell you—just go for it. Tattoo that on your forehead, people! Shout it from the rooftops. Nike is not the best-selling brand of sneakers for nothing! Attempt to tackle the trials you do not consider yourself to be capable of whether it be saving enough money for a car, DMing your crush, writing that pilot for a TV show, going to an open mic and cracking some jokes, running a marathon, taking a dance lesson, whatever it may be that has been on your heart, JUST DO IT. Give that tiny bitch devil on your shoulder the finger and tell him your friend Rachel says to fuck off.

Game On, Motherfucker.

Hell yes, we're playing games.
Feel free to add alcohol (21+).
We could all use it after two hundred pages of my bullshit.

Fuck, Marry, Kill.
You know what to do, GO!

Adrenaline Guy: F M K

My ex (Tyler): F M K

Homeboy: F M K

.

Place That Sub-Tweet:
This one requires a bit more thought.
What the hell was I thinking when I mindlessly launched
these tweets out into the abyss?

Rach
@rachelhospers

Jon Hamm- evidence that God is a
woman

1. Where was I when I tweeted this?
   a. At home watching *Mad Men*
   b. At a rooftop bar, tipsy off red
      wine
   c. In the cologne aisle of
      Nordstrom
   d. In bed alone

Rach
@rachelhospers

I survive on the breath you are finished
with

2. Why did I tweet this John Mayer
   lyric?
   a. I was missing my ex
   b. I was jamming to "Heavier
      Things" alone in my
      apartment
   c. Adrenaline Guy said one
      thing that indicated that
      he might care about me the
      night prior
   d. I had a really intense
      conversation with a new guy
      via Instagram DM

Rach
@rachelhospers

Last night in my dream someone asked
me what love was and I couldn't give
them a straight answer. I've been all
sorts of fucked up since.

3. How long after Tyler and I broke
   up did I tweet this?
   a. 3 days
   b. 2.5 weeks
   c. A month and a half
   d. A year

Rach 🔒
@rachelhospers

Boys suck so I'm treating myself to sleeping with the air conditioning on tonight

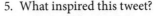

<   **Tweet**

Rach 🔒
@rachelhospers

Eye contact makes me uncomfortable let's talk about it

<   **Tweet**

Rach 🔒
@rachelhospers

The world is ending so fuck it I'm not paying my credit card bill anymore

<   **Tweet**

Rach 🔒
@rachelhospers

Rescue dogs, not men :)

4. Why was I pissed?
   a. A guy ghosted me
   b. I was out at a bar and the guy I thought was cute never introduced himself even though his only cue from me was dodgy eye contact
   c. I did not get enough likes on my thirst trap
   d. The guy I had my eye on got back together with his ex

5. What inspired this tweet?
   a. A customer asking me questions at work
   b. A Bumble date
   c. Me ordering a smoothie
   d. A dude telling me to look into his eyes during sex

6. What was going on in America when I tweeted this?
   a. The border crisis
   b. Abortion rights being threatened in some states
   c. Climate change
   d. All of the above

7. How old was I when I discovered that I had a savior complex?
   a. 20
   b. 21
   c. 22
   d. 23

Answers: B, C, D, D, C

217

Honest Hinge Profile:

What would our Hinge profiles look like if we were one hundred percent ourselves?

In case you have never used Hinge, they have these corny question prompts for you to fill out and add to your profile.

This is what mine would look like if I truly wanted to die alone:

7:34	Cancel **Write Answer** Done

My favorite thing to do alone is ✏

Everything|

9:53	Cancel **Write Answer** Done

I want someone who ✏

Hates me a little bit

7:54	Cancel **Write Answer** Done

I go crazy for ✏

Facial hair, tattoos and unaddressed emotional trauma|

7:40	Cancel **Write Answer** Done

Let's make sure we're on the same page about ✏

Me being the hot one in the relationship|

7:52	Cancel **Write Answer** Done

I bet you can't ✏

Make me cum

Okay you get the idea … your turn! You've got one hundred
and fifty characters.
Do your worst, then tweet them at me!

8:32 ⬙ ▪▪▪ 🔋 **Write Answer**	8:34 ⬙ ▪▪▪ 🔋 **Write Answer**
Cancel **Write Answer** Done	Cancel **Write Answer** Done
You should *not* go out with me if ✎	The secret to getting to know me is ✎
Enter your answer here	Enter your answer here
150	
8:32 ⬙ ▪▪▪ 🔋 **Write Answer**	8:33 ⬙ ▪▪▪ 🔋 **Write Answer**
Cancel **Write Answer** Done	Cancel **Write Answer** Done
The sign of a great first date ✎	Don't hate me if I ✎
Enter your answer here	Enter your answer here
8:33 ⬙ ▪▪▪ 🔋 **Write Answer**	8:34 ⬙ ▪▪▪ 🔋 **Write Answer**
Cancel **Write Answer** Done	Cancel **Write Answer** Done
You'll know I like you if ✎	The one thing I'd love to know about you is ✎
Enter your answer here	Enter your answer here

Acknowledgments

Thank you so much for reading my book. It means the world to me that you would spend this time with me. To be quite honest, writing this book gave me purpose and saved me on some really tough days, so thank you for granting me a platform. I hope you have found some joy here. My wish is for all of my readers to love themselves fiercely. I picture you cuties all cuddled up on your couches with my book and some Postmates from your favorite local joint. I hope you treat yourself to something yummy. I hope you laugh out loud. I hope you find your soul mates and hold them tight. I hope you look within and find the truest soul mate of all—you. *Of course* I had to throw some more cheese at you. We both know you love it.

Thank you again to my friends who encouraged me throughout this process and did not unfollow me when I tweeted that I was crying at my book again. Without those telling me they could not wait to read what I wrote and that they were excited for me, I might have never scraped up the motivation to get this thing made.

To the romantic partners I have mentioned in this book, thank you for being my muses, you sexy little thangs.

Thank you to my parents, my soul mates, my friends, and to the rest of my family. This sounds dramatic, but it is true: you keep me alive and healthy. I hope I did not embarrass you too much.

To dance, thank you for being my everything.

And finally, to you, Rach. We fucking did it.

References

Moody Bitches: The Truth About the Drugs You're Taking, the Sleep You're Missing, the Sex You're Not Having, and What's Really Making You Crazy by Julie Holland

Women Who Love Too Much by Robin Norwood

Codependent No More by Melody Beattie

The Body Keeps the Score: Brain, Mind, and Body in the Healing of Trauma by Bessel Van Der Kolk

Codependency vs Boundaries Chart by Courtney Burg

Conquering Panic and Anxiety Disorders: Success Stories, Strategies and Other Good News edited by Jenna Glatzer with commentary by Paul Foxman

10% Happier: How I Tamed the Voice in My Head, Reduced Stress Without Losing My Edge, and Found Self-Help That Actually Works—A True Story by Dan Harris

"Joe Rogan Experience" #1109 with Dr. Matthew Walker

"Amy" (2015) Directed by Asif Kapadia

World Health Organization (www.who.int)

Recommendations

The War of Art: Break Through the Blocks and Win Your Inner Creative Battles by Steven Pressfield

You Are a Badass: How to Stop Doubting Your Greatness and Start Living an Awesome Life by Jen Sincero

F*cked: Being Sexually Explorative and Self-Confident in a World That's Screwed by Corinne Fisher and Krystyna Hutchinson

No Hard Feelings: Poems and Stories by Thom Henke

Life Without Ed: How One Woman Declared Independence from Her Eating Disorder and How You Can Too by Jenni Schaefer

I'm Fine...And Other Lies by Whitney Cummings

Steal Like An Artist: 10 Things Nobody Told You About Being Creative by Austin Kleon

The Four Agreements: A Practical Guide to Personal Freedom by Don Miguel Ruiz

Resources

Substance Abuse and Mental Health Services Administration
SAMHSA's National Helpline: 1-800-662-HELP (4357)

National Eating Disorders Association
NEDA's Helpline: 1-800-931-2237

National Suicide Prevention Lifeline
1-800-273-8255

The National Sexual Assault Hotline
1-800-656-HOPE (4673)

Safe Horizon www.safehorizon.org
1-800-621-HOPE (4673)

CPSIA information can be obtained
at www.ICGtesting.com
Printed in the USA
LVHW081719100220
646428LV00012B/242/J